About the Book

Presenting a fascinating array of facts and folklore, Peter Limburg traces the name origins of forty-eight familiar birds found in North America. With a keen sense for the unusual, he relates a wide variety of legends, superstitions, and anecdotes connected with the bird and its name. We learn the background of such familiar expressions as "the bluebird of happiness," "talking turkey," and "cooking his goose." A discussion of the territory, nesting, and feeding habits and instincts peculiar to the bird is part of each entry.

This is a delightful potpourri of information. Peter Limburg is an avid etymologist who will infect his readers with a wonderful enthusiasm for words and their origins. Accurate drawings of each bird and lighthearted picture interpretations of the text by Tom Huffman decorate the book from beginning to end.

*To my daughter Ellen,
who loves birds*

What's-in-the-Names of

BIRDS

by Peter Limburg

illustrated by Tom Huffman

Text copyright © 1975 by Peter R. Limburg
Illustrations copyright © 1975 by Thomas Huffman
All rights reserved. This book, or parts thereof, may not
be reproduced in any form without permission in writing from
the publishers. Published simultaneously in
Canada by Longman Canada Limited, Toronto.
SBN: GB-698-30515-9
SBN: TR-698-20263-5
Library of Congress Catalog Card Number: 72-94142
PRINTED IN THE UNITED STATES OF AMERICA
10 up

Coward, McCann & Geoghegan, Inc.
New York

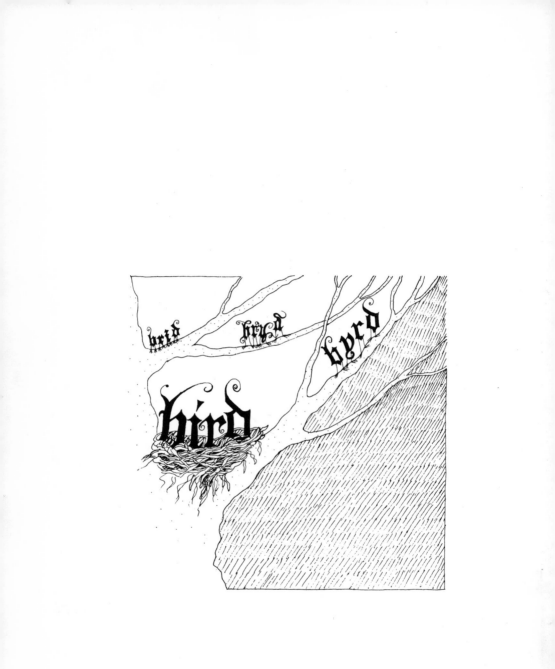

BIRD

Bird comes from the Anglo-Saxon *brid*, which meant the young of birds, from a sparrow to an eagle. Adult birds in Anglo-Saxon days were called fowls. Between about 1150 and 1500, the *brid* turned into *bryd*, then *byrd*, and finally *bird*. By then it had pretty much taken on its modern sense of any feathered animal, young or old. Some people made a distinction between "fowl" and "bird" as late as the mid-1700's, saying "fowl" for a large bird and "bird" for a small one. Nowadays "fowl" refers only to barnyard birds, particularly chickens, unless otherwise qualified.

Birds branched off from reptiles about 140,000,000 years ago. The oldest known bird was found as a fossil in a slate quarry in Germany in 1861. It looked like a slender, long-fingered lizard, except that the stone bore the unmistakable prints of feathers! Here was something to startle the scientists and back up Charles Darwin's shocking new theory of evolution. It was given the name of *archaeopteryx*, Greek for "ancient wing." Archaeopteryx had a long, lizardlike tail and jaws full of sharp teeth. Its wings had claws at the outer joint. (Only one species of bird living today has functional wing claws—the strange hoatzin of South America—and they drop off when the bird is only a few weeks old.) Archaeopteryx was probably a poor flier, if it could actually fly at all. Judging from its skeleton (only three have been found), it probably spent most of its time running along the ground on its strong hind legs or climbing up trees and rocks with the help of its wing claws. From these high points it could glide down or perhaps flap for a short distance.

Today's birds have come a long way from the primitive archaeopteryx. They have evolved into beautifully designed machines for flying, swimming, or whatever else their way of life calls for. Birds have moved into every niche that nature offers, from desert to swampland, from arctic cold to tropical heat, everywhere except the bottom of the ocean, for all birds are air breathers. They eat seeds, leaves, fruits, acorns, insects, microscopic water organisms, fish, reptiles, mammals, and each other. They pick up sticks and pebbles, crack nuts, tear flesh, spear fish, and chisel holes in wood with their lips, for this is what their bills are—the skin of the lips has turned into a horny substance and taken on special shapes for these tasks. But with all their specialization, birds still lay eggs like reptiles.

It is feathers that distinguish birds from all other living creatures. All birds have feathers, and no other animals do. The feather is actually a highly specialized skin scale, composed of a central shaft with hundreds of filaments standing out from it, held together by an intricate arrangement of barbs and hooks. Feathers give the bird's wing great lifting surface with little weight. They can have their angle altered to control flight. They can be fluffed up to trap air and insulate the bird in cold weather. And they provide a protective coat that is better than fur.

Not all birds can fly. Some, like the ostrich, have grown so big that wings could not lift them, and they have become runners on the surface of the earth instead. Their unused wings have become shrunken and useless. Some swimming birds, like the penguins, have also lost the power of flight, although scientists who filmed penguins with underwater cameras found that they actually do fly in the water. But most birds fly, even if not very well. And some fly superlatively.

How intelligent are birds? By and large, they seem pretty stupid from the human viewpoint. Indeed, "bird-brained" has been a synonym for "stupid" for many years. But scientists tell us that birds are "bird-brained" by necessity. Their largely airborne way of life and the need to avoid predators and catch their own prey mean that they must react with lightning speed to things that happen around them, without taking time to think. As a result, birds are governed mainly by instinct and reflex. They are rather like feathered computers reacting automatically to data that are fed into them. From the viewpoint of survival, this has worked well enough so that few birds have needed to develop reasoning power. Even the ways they court each other and take care of their young are programmed into them.

Primitive man felt there was something magical about birds, those creatures that could soar in the air where no others could follow. He often worshiped them as gods. Later, as men grew more sophisticated, they made some birds sacred to their gods. They believed that birds could make thunder and bring rain, foretell death, tell fortunes, and bring good or bad luck. Many of these beliefs lived on as superstitions until modern times, and uneducated people still believe some of them.

Man has hunted birds for food since prehistoric days. Before the beginning of history he also learned to tame some of them. This gave him a supply of meat and eggs always on hand. Today the production of certain birds for food, like chickens, turkeys, and ducks, is a major industry in many parts of the world.

Birds have given us many proverbs and expressions, such as "A bird in the hand is worth two in the bush." The Italians say, "Better an egg today than a hen tomorrow," and the Germans say, "Better a sparrow in the hand than a stork on the roof." All of them mean that you are better off with what you have than with something more alluring that is not within your reach.

"Birds of a feather flock together" dates from the late 1500's. It originally referred to criminals from the same gang, and it has always kept a meaning of disapproval.

"Bird" to mean a girl is not modern slang. It goes back to the Middle Ages. But then it was a tender, respectful term, and today it is definitely not.

A "bird's-eye view" is a view from high up, such as only birds could have before balloons and airplanes were invented (unless you climbed a very tall church steeple or stood on the edge of a high cliff). It is still used in the sense of giving someone the whole picture of a situation in a few words.

When nineteenth-century British audiences disliked an actor, they would give him the "big bird" and hiss him loudly. This expression supposedly came from the loud hissing of angry geese, which are pretty big birds. Americans took over the expression, but our "bird" of disapproval is not a hiss but the rude noise also known as the "raspberry" or the "Bronx cheer."

With thousands of birds to choose from, many with interesting stories about their names or about the birds themselves, why were these particular birds chosen? Why is the robin, for instance, covered in this book while the penguin is not?

It seemed like a good idea to devote this book to birds that are either native to North America or have established themselves firmly here. The robin is a native North American bird, while the lovable penguin can exist here only at zoos and aquariums, where its special needs are taken care of. The starling is a native of Europe, but it is now so firmly established here that it cannot be gotten rid of, no matter how much we would like to.

Many of the birds that appear in this book are also native to Europe, and their names were given to them there. Some do not exist in Europe but were given the names of European birds by early settlers who thought that they resembled those birds—which they often did only by a wide, wide stretch of the imagination.

Some interesting native birds, like the cranes, have been left out because they are rare, and our aim has been to include birds that are common enough so that readers may hope to catch at least a glimpse of most of them.

We hope that this book will not earn a "big bird" but will set our readers' curiosity soaring and make them want to learn more about those fascinating feathered creatures, the birds.

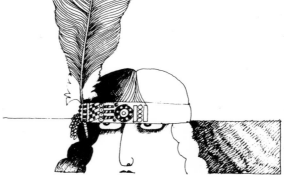

BLACKBIRD

In Europe there lives a black thrush which the Anglo-Saxons used to call an *osle*. Then it was called an *ousel*. Toward the end of the 1400's people stopped calling this black bird an ousel and called it simply *blackbird*.

English settlers in America found birds that looked very much like the familiar blackbirds of England, although they were a bit smaller and some had colorful markings that the English birds didn't have. So they called them blackbirds, too. American and European blackbirds are not related, but this fact was only discovered well after the name had become firmly established.

There are five kinds of blackbirds in North America. In each, only the males are black; the females have streaky, brown plumage that makes a good camouflage as they sit on the nest. Two of the blackbirds are all black. One variety has a yellow head and throat. The most familiar kinds have red shoulder patches: the red-winged blackbird and the tricolored blackbird. The two look almost identical, except that the redwing has a buff stripe at the edge of its shoulder patch, and the tricolored has a white stripe. One calls "Cong-ka-ree!" and the other "O-ka-lee!" Neither is a good singer.

Blackbirds come north in early spring and stake out nesting territories in swamps and marshes. After the young are able to take care of themselves, the birds migrate south to their wintering grounds, forming huge flocks. A flock of several hundred thousand blackbirds is not at all unusual, and some roosting sites in the South are home for 5,000,000 or so birds. Needless to say, the hungry birds do tremendous damage as they feed on farm crops. Birds from a big flock often fly as far as fifty miles from the roost to find food. When they return at dusk, they make an aerial traffic jam worse than any auto highway at rush hour. It may take four hours or more before the last birds are settled down for the night.

In bygone days, Europeans used to trap small birds and eat them. The blackbird was one that often ended up on the table, roasted or baked in a pie. So the old rhyme, "Sing a song of sixpence/ A pocketful of rye/ Four and twenty blackbirds/ Baked in a pie," didn't seem any stranger to sixteenth-century Englishmen than "four and twenty cheeseburgers" would seem to us. It seems also that kings and other important people sometimes had live blackbirds hidden in an empty pie shell. When the pie was cut open, the

birds would fly out and flutter wildly around the dining room, causing no end of amusement to the guests as they knocked over wine cups, put out candles, and in general created pandemonium.

Some scholars claim that the rhyme was really a political attack on King Henry VIII, disguised as an innocent children's rhyme. The "blackbirds" were supposed to be the deeds of ownership to twenty-four manors that Henry had seized for himself.

"Black" comes from the Anglo-Saxon word *blaec* or *blac*. It was often confused with another *blac* which meant "pale" or "white." The two words were straightened out hundreds of years ago, and now nobody would wonder if a blackbird was black or white.

BLUEBIRD

The bluebird is a true native North American bird. It does not exist in any other part of the world. European settlers in America had never seen anything like a bluebird before, and they had no name for the handsome little bird with the bright blue head and back and the rusty-red breast. So they named it for its color.

Bluebirds belong to the thrush family, and there are three species of them: the eastern bluebird, the one the early colonists named; the western bluebird; and the mountain bluebird, which is the bluest of them all, as the males are blue all over. (Female bluebirds have blue only in their wings.) Between them, the bluebirds cover all the forty-eight mainland United States, the southern and western fringes of Canada, and a part of Alaska. They also range down into Mexico. Four states have the bluebird as their state bird: Idaho, Missouri, Nevada, and New York.

Bluebirds, which live on soft-bodied insects and fruits, have slender bills. They often perch on a twig with their bills pointed down and their shoulders hunched up, as if ready to dive into action. That is just what they are doing, for they are scanning the ground for insects to pounce on. Bluebirds are gentle, unaggressive birds. They do not push other birds out of the way at the backyard bird feeder or rob their nests of eggs and young. But they are scrappy little fighters when threatened, and they can put to flight a bullying jay or starling much larger than themselves.

Unlike the loon, the owl, the turkey, and other native birds, the bluebird did not play a large role in Indian myths. And, not being known in Europe, it could not get a part in any European myths or folklore—not until 1909, when a Belgian named Maurice Maeterlinck wrote a hit play called *The Blue Bird*. In this play, which was filled with strange symbolism, a pair of small children set out to search for the mysterious Blue Bird of Happiness, but they never catch it. Why Maeterlinck should have picked a bluebird as his symbol of happiness is a mystery, since he probably never saw one in his life. But blue is a very symbolic color. To modern Americans, "the blues" stands for the essence of sadness and misery; in earlier times blue, the color of the sky, was the color of hope. It was also the color of faithfulness and loyalty, from which comes the phrase "true blue." To the Cherokee Indians, blue was the color of the north, and it also meant trouble. Blue is a traditional color for the edges of Jewish prayer shawls, and in Roman Catholic tradition, it belongs to the Virgin Mary. Since Maeterlinck was fascinated by symbols, he must have been thinking of some of these things.

Maeterlinck wrote more than two dozen plays and books during his long life (he died in 1949 at the age of eighty-seven). But the most famous was *The Blue Bird*. He also wrote important books about bees and termites, for one of his hobbies was the study of insects.

Bluebirds were once as common as robins in the eastern United States, but now they are quite rare. One reason is that they used to nest in holes in trees, particularly old apple trees in orchards. The building boom that covered much of the United States and Canada with suburbs where once there had been farms and woodland destroyed most of the bluebirds' nesting grounds. Another reason is widespread spraying with chemical pesticides (bug killers), which also poisoned the bluebirds which fed on the insects.

Homeowners can help bring the bluebird back by limiting the amount of chemical pesticides they use and, even more important, by providing nesting boxes for the birds to take the place of the trees that were destroyed to make room for houses. A bluebird house should have an entrance hole just 1½ inches in diameter—if it is any smaller, the bluebirds couldn't get in, and if it is larger, nest raiders like starlings and jays might force their way in. The nest box should also be at least 6 inches deep to keep starlings from reaching the eggs or baby bluebirds by poking their heads in. The nest box can be mounted on a tree or a pole, preferably with the entrance facing south.

BLUE JAY

This noisy bully of the bird feeder and robber of other birds'
nests was named for his bright-blue crest, back, and wings.
The "jay" part of his name tells of his family relationships,
for he belongs to a subdivision of the crow family known as
the jays.

"Jay" is an Old French name that was taken into English.
It comes from the Latin *gaius* or *gaia*, which originally
meant the noisy, chattering Eurasian jay, a gray, black, and

white bird with blue wing patches but without a crest. Gaius was a popular Roman man's name which may have been given as a nickname to the bird, as Robin was given to the redbreast.

The blue jay is one of the few colorful birds that stays in the northern states during the winter. One reason may be that the jay is such an adaptable and resourceful bird. Jays will eat almost anything, and when one source of food runs out, they turn to another. They have found good pickings in suburban backyards and city parks. The blue jay is common over the United States as far west as the Rockies. Six other species of jays inhabit North America, mostly in the West and Southwest. The gray jay, or Canada jay, lives in the pine and spruce forests of Canada and the northwestern United States. It often hangs around lumber camps, cadging food scraps from the lumberjacks and becoming very tame. Campers and hikers also get visits from this bold panhandler, which is truthfully nicknamed the "camp robber."

All the jays are thievish, at least by man's standards. The blue jay not only robs the nests of other birds, but also raids farms and gardens, devouring newly planted corn and other seeds and gobbling up ripening fruit or ruining it by pecking holes in it. Old-time farmers swore at the jay and called him "corn thief."

During nesting season, angrily screaming small birds can be seen chasing blue jays away from their eggs and young. Blue jays themselves gang up to harass a marauding hawk or owl, for they are not without courage. They often (unintentionally) save the lives of other birds and animals by screaming an alarm when they spot a hunter. Blue jays also do some good by eating insects and grubs.

Blue jays are good mimics, and they can do a very convincing imitation of the scream of a red-shouldered hawk. This terrifies all other birds within hearing distance and sends them into a panic. Old-time naturalists were convinced that the blue jay gets a malicious pleasure from its trick.

BUZZARD

In the United States a buzzard is a vulture, circling lazily in the sky and looking for dead animals to eat. In Britain, where the name originated, a buzzard is a kind of hawk.

The buzzard's name comes from the Old French *busart*, which comes from *buteo*, the Latin name for a kind of broad-winged hawk. The name had taken hold in England by the 1200's. The English buzzard was—and is—a slow-flying, clumsy hawk, utterly useless for hunting. (In the Middle Ages, hunting birds and small mammals with trained hawks was a popular sport.) So the buzzard came to be regarded with contempt. A hundred years before Shakespeare was born, Englishmen were using "buzzard" as a title of disgrace for a no-good, ignorant, or stupid person. Dictionaries used to define the buzzard as "a useless hawk." (Actually, buzzard hawks do some good by eating mice and insects, in addition to their other prey.)

Settlers in the American colonies transferred the name of "buzzard" to the native vultures. Perhaps the vultures, in flight, reminded them of English buzzard hawks. Perhaps the contempt they had for buzzard hawks made them think that "buzzard" was a good name for a carrion-eating vulture.

There are two birds in the United States that are called buzzards. One is the turkey vulture, which ranges over the whole country and up into Canada in the summer. The other is the black vulture, which lives mostly in the South.

Country people in the South used to say that when the turkey buzzards came back after the winter, there would be no more frost, and it was safe to plant crops. Some believed that wearing a feather of a black buzzard in their hair would prevent rheumatism. The aged, bent nearly double from the pain of rheumatism, would still insist that their buzzard feathers had done them more good than all the medicines they had got from doctors. At that, the buzzard feathers were probably just as good a "cure" as the other folk remedies that float around.

CANARY

The canary is named for the Canary Islands, the home of its wild ancestors. It was the Romans who named this cluster of volcanic peaks that rise out of the ocean off the northwest coast of Africa. Explorers who had reached the islands— probably around the beginning of the Christian Era— brought back reports of the big native dogs that roamed them. So Roman geographers named them *Insulae Canariae*, the "Dog Islands," from *canis*, meaning "dog."

Spanish fortune hunters conquered the islands during the 1400's, wiping out most of the native population in doing so. On the islands they found small wild finches that sang pleasingly, so they took some back to the mainland as cage birds. From these birds the modern canaries are descended.

The original canaries were a dull olive-green on top, streaked with black and brown; below, they were greenish yellow. Centuries of selective breeding gave us the familiar bright yellow canary. Canary breeders also improved the canary's singing voice, so that a modern canary can produce melodies that a wild canary would never dream of.

Canaries were first imported into Europe in the 1500's. The name "canary bird" first appeared in English in 1576, when Shakespeare was a boy of twelve. Eventually canary birds became so familiar that people simply dropped the "bird."

Germany became a center for the breeding of canaries and training them to sing. The people of the Harz Mountain region were the greatest specialists in canary breeding, and the finest ones still come from there.

The native American goldfinches are often called wild canaries because of the males' brilliant yellow plumage in breeding season. However, they are not closely related to the true canaries, and they do not sing nearly as well as the wild finches of the Canary Islands.

In bygone years, canaries were used as gas detectors in coal mines. The little birds are much more sensitive than human beings to poisonous gases and pass out much sooner. Miners took a canary along with them when they went down to the coal seam and frequently checked the cage. If the canary acted drowsy or lay unconscious on the floor of its

cage, it was a signal to leave the mine shaft, because deadly gases were building up.

Luxurious hotels used to keep cages full of canaries hanging high up near the ceilings of their lounges and dining rooms, to entertain the guests with their twitterings and songs. While the canaries would doubtless rather have been free if they had their choice, it was still a better life than being down in a coal mine.

CARDINAL

The cardinal is named for the cardinals of the Roman Catholic Church, whose red robes its plumage resembles. "Cardinal" comes from the Latin *cardinalis*, which comes from the word *cardo*, meaning "hinge." *Cardinalis* therefore came to carry the meaning of "so important that everything else hinges on it." As the Roman Catholic Church grew and became more highly organized, the title of Cardinal was given to some of the most important senior officials. The cardinals, also known as "princes of the church," rank next to the Pope in importance. As a mark of their high rank they wear brilliant red robes.

Early settlers in the Southern colonies saw a bright-red bird with an imposing crest strutting gravely about on the ground and nicknamed him cardinal bird. The name stuck; in fact, even today some people say "cardinal bird," although most people have dropped the "bird." Other names for the cardinal include redbird, Virginia cardinal, and Kentucky cardinal. Dictionaries tell us that the bird is also known as cardinal finch (an accurate description, since the cardinal belongs to the finch family) and cardinal grosbeak (cardinals and grosbeaks are closely related). One of the oddest names for the cardinal is Virginia nightingale, odd because the nightingale is famous for its beautiful melodies and the cardinal's song is a monotonous "Cheer! Cheer! Cheer!"

As some of these nicknames indicate, the cardinal was known as a Southern bird. In fact, it used to be as much a symbol of the South as cottonfields, magnolia trees, and stately plantation houses. But nowadays, with backyard bird feeders providing a winter food supply, cardinals have moved into the North as well. They are shy birds and don't like to come near houses, but when they are hungry enough, they will come quite close. Cardinals will seldom fly up onto a feeder. They prefer to eat on the ground, picking up the seeds spilled by other birds.

The female cardinal is not brilliantly dressed as is the male. She is a dull olive-gray except for her bright red-orange bill and dull red trim on her wings and tail. This coloring is such an effective camouflage that it is often impossible to see a female cardinal perched on a bush or tree until she moves.

The colors of the cardinals tell an interesting story in themselves. The male's red is brightest on the head and

breast, helping him flash a warning signal to rival males. He is duller on his back and wings, probably helping to shield him from predators as he flies around his territory foraging for food for his mate and young ones. The female's dull coloring lets her sit on the nest almost unseen. This difference in coloring is often found when the female bird does all the incubating of the eggs and the male goes out to gather food. When both birds share both tasks, the male and female look much more alike.

The cardinal is the leading state bird in the United States. Seven states have chosen it as their emblem: Illinois, Indiana, Kentucky, North Carolina, Ohio, Virginia, and West Virginia. And one of the great baseball teams—the St. Louis Cardinals—is also named for the cheerful redbird.

CHICKADEE

Named for its cheery call, the chickadee is one of the birds
most often seen in winter in the northern United States. To
old-time New England farmers, the chickadee's mating song
was one of the earliest signs that spring was coming. Some
people claimed that the birds really sang "Sweet weather!"
or "Spring soon!" People liked their friendliness toward humans and appreciated the fact that they didn't go south to a
milder region in winter. Perhaps for these reasons the chickadee was chosen as the state bird of Massachusetts and
Maine.

There are seven kinds of chickadees in North America, but the most common and by far the most widespread is the black-capped chickadee, the state bird of the two New England states. All of them are little birds, between four and five inches long.

Chickadees belong to the titmouse family, and they often flock together with tufted titmice. This may be because the two birds eat the same kinds of food—seeds and insects—and by watching each other, they can learn where the food is. And both chickadees and titmice are sociable birds anyway.

"Titmouse" was once titmose, *tit* being a folksy fourteenth-century English name for anything little, and *mose* being a general sort of name for small, dull-colored birds. But words have a way of losing their meanings, and over the next couple of hundred years Englishmen forgot that *mose* ever had a meaning of its own. In fact, they thought it must be a strange, old-fashioned form of "mouse." And most birds of the titmouse family *are* mousy-looking, with their dull gray and brownish colors. So the bird became "titmouse" about a hundred years after Columbus reached the New World, and that has been its name ever since.

CHICKEN

Chicken comes from the Anglo-Saxon *cicen*, which originally meant the young of the domestic fowl we now call the chicken. *Cicen* also referred to the meat of these young domestic fowls. "Fowl" comes from the Anglo-Saxon word *fugol*, which originally meant "bird." "Chicken" was prized as a delicate dish because the young, tender chicks were much, much easier to eat than the tough, older "fowls." Clever innkeepers caught on to the trick of serving up fowl and calling it chicken to sound more appetizing. It is hard to say just when this deception began, but "chicken" took the place of "fowl" at restaurants and as the general term for chicken meat more than a century ago. By then people were also calling the birds chickens.

"Hen" comes from the Anglo-Saxon *henn*, the female form of *hana*, or rooster. The male chicken is known in the United States as a rooster, and in most other English-speaking countries as a cock, a name which is probably an imitation of the bird's clucking. "Cock" was also the commonly used term in the United States until well into the 1800's. But then a mania for "respectability" swept over the nation. Since "cock" also had a highly improper slang meaning, the word was banned from polite conversation, and no decent person would let it sully his lips. In its place they used an old dialect word, "rooster"—the one who "rules the roost." (For those readers who have never seen an old-time hen house, the roost was a pole that ran from one wall to the other, a few feet off the floor. The hens and their mate would flap up to it at night and sleep perched on it.)

All the hundreds of breeds of domestic chickens are descended from the wild jungle fowl of southeast Asia and India, which is one of the pheasant clan. The chicken's other relatives include the turkey, guinea hen, megapode, grouse, partridge, peacock, quail, and others. All of them together are known to ornithologists by the imposing name of Galliformes, or "fowl-shaped birds," from *gallus*, the Latin word for "rooster."

The chicken was one of the first birds, if not the very first, to be domesticated by man. Fossil chicken bones more than 4,000 years old have been found around the remains of prehistoric villages. Scientists think that chickens were probably first kept for religious purposes, such as sacrifices to the sun, for the cock's habit of crowing at daybreak made him a symbol of the sun. Chickens were also fertility symbols. In

31

time, people began to eat the eggs of the sacred fowls and then the extra fowls that were not needed for religious ceremonies.

The sacred character of the chicken lingered for many centuries. The Greeks and Romans sacrificed chickens to their gods, and the Romans kept special chickens for prophesying the outcome of a battle and other important events. Priests would invoke the deities and then throw grain to the chickens. If the chickens ate heartily, it was a sign that the gods were favorable. If they picked at their food listlessly or turned up their beaks at it, the gods were angry, and any action taken would end in disaster. Not everyone took this belief seriously. One famous Roman general carried his own sacred chickens around with him, and he starved them for a day beforehand each time he had to consult the gods about a battle. The chickens naturally ate well, and the omens were favorable.

Chickens were almost ideal domestic animals, especially for primitive peoples. Their crowing at daybreak woke people up to begin the daily chores. They pretty much took care of themselves, for they are natural scavengers. With a little protection against foxes, hawks, and other predators they not only survived but increased. They gave eggs, meat (usually when they were too old to lay anymore), and feathers, which in cold countries could be used to stuff quilts. As civilizations developed, man took better care of his chickens, feeding them, sheltering them, and breeding them to lay more eggs, to grow bigger and meatier, and for other things that man desired.

Fed and protected by man, chickens did not need their intelligence, and they became proverbial for their stupidity. They also became symbols of cowardice, as in "chicken-hearted" and its modern variation, "chicken." At the same time, the fighting cock, specially bred for combat, was a symbol of fierceness and bravery. A stupid, conceited man used to be called a coxcomb. These are a few of the many expressions in which chickens figure. Of course, we should not forget "cocktail," a mixed drink with liquor in it. "Cocktail" supposedly originated as the name of a mixed drink invented during the Revolutionary War and decorated with a rooster's tail feather stuck in the glass.

The chicken is the symbolic bird of two states, Delaware and Rhode Island. It is also one of the ancient symbols of France. The Roman name for the ancient inhabitants of France was *Galli* (in English, Gauls), and the name for the country of the Galli was *Gallia*. Since the Roman name for the rooster was *gallus*, the French adopted the ground fighting cock as a symbol of French valor.

CROW

The crow was originally "the bird that crows," for its name comes from an old Anglo-Saxon word meaning "to crow." This word was *crawan,* and the bird's name in Anglo-Saxon England was *crawe.* (Crowing, strictly speaking, meant the loud noise made by a rooster; but it also came to include any long, loud call made by a bird.) Some related names for the crow in other languages are German *Krähe* (pronounced KRAY-heh), Swedish kråka (pronounced CROW-kah), and Dutch *kraai* (pronounced CRY). All these names suggest the harsh cawing of a crow. The Romans called the crow *cornix* or *corvus,* which turn up in scientific names for the various crow species. *Cornix cornicatur* was how a Roman would say, "The crow is cawing."

Despite its harsh, unmusical voice, the crow is classified as a songbird because of the structure of its voice box. Some naturalists claim that crows actually do sing in a soft, musical voice when they think they are absolutely alone, but this would be very hard to prove, especially since crows are extremely wary birds and can spot an intruder at the drop of a feather.

Crows belong to a large family of birds, which includes the magpies, jays, and nutcrackers. Distant relatives are the beautiful birds of paradise of New Guinea and Australia.

Crows are intelligent, adaptable birds, and they have spread over most parts of the world except South America and Antarctica. They eat almost anything, from carrion to fruit. They are known for robbing other birds' nests of eggs and young, and they sometimes eat mice, frogs, and crayfish. Farmers hate crows because they eat newly planted corn and other grains, and they have a distressing fondness for nibbling on ears of corn while they are on the plants. Crows also prey on baby chickens if they are allowed to run out in the open. On the other hand, they do some good by eating harmful insects and grubs.

It is hard for man to measure the intelligence of a non-human creature like a crow, but tests have shown that crows can count up to three or four, and captive crows can learn the meanings of some human words, especially if they have to do with food or eating. Hunters know that crows can count because they cannot be fooled by three hunters entering a blind to hide and one or two leaving. The crows know there is still one man with a gun inside. They also recognize guns, for they are bold around unarmed humans, but the sight of a person with a gun sends them fleeing with loud alarm calls. The alarm call is just one of many calls that crows have, for they have (for birds) quite a complex language that can convey a number of meanings. There is a "here I am" call, an assembly call to summon a mob of crows to attack an enemy such as an owl or hawk, a mating call,

and so on. But the best proof of crows' intelligence is the way they manage to outwit man and make a good living off him.

There are five species of crows in North America, counting the raven, which is the largest of the crows. By far the commonest and best known is the common crow, which is found over almost all of the United States and ranges far up into Canada in summer. It is a good-sized bird, reaching nearly a foot and a half in length. In flight, crows look rather like hawks, but they can be told apart because crows spend most of their time flapping their wings to keep airborne, while hawks spend most of their time soaring. Many small birds react to the sight of a crow with the same fear they would have for a hawk. But a common sight in spring and early summer is a small bird angrily chasing a marauding crow away from its nest. The parental instinct gives the little bird courage to defend its offspring, while the crow, which is not defending anything, reacts by running away from the little nuisance that is trying to peck it.

Sometimes a flock of crows can be heard making a dreadful racket. Then the flock will suddenly turn on one of its members and peck the luckless bird to death. Country people believed that the victim was a crow sentinel that had failed in its duty and been tried and executed by its mates. Crows do set out sentinel birds when a flock is raiding a farmer's grainfield or orchard, but these gangland-style executions are certainly not the result of a trial. Crows have neither the reasoning power nor the language for that. But animals that live in groups often turn on one of their mates that is sick or injured, and this is what probably happens with the crows.

There are many superstitions about crows. Some have to do with the weather—crows are supposed to predict tornadoes and rain by the way they fly. Some have to do with magic; for example, finding a dead crow in the road is supposed to mean good luck. These beliefs come from pagan times, when crows were thought to be associated with gods and demons.

The crow was a leading character in many folktales and fables, and has given many picturesque phrases to the English language. "As the crow flies," means the shortest distance between two points, for the crow could fly straight through the air, while a human being on the ground must make many twists and turns and detours to get around obstacles. So from Circleville to Centerville might be ten miles as the crow flies, but thirty-five by road.

"I have a crow to pick with you" means "I have some unpleasant business to settle with you." Shakespeare used this expression in one of his plays. Nowadays it is not used— we pick bones instead of crows.

To "eat crow" means to make a very humiliating apology, for old crows are tough and bad-flavored and hard to choke down. Young crows, however, are supposed to make good eating.

The "crow's nest" was a small lookout platform high on the mast of a sailing ship. It was named from the crow's habit of building its nest high up in a tall tree.

CUCKOO

To the Romans, the cuckoo was a *cuculus*, to the Greeks, a *kokkyx*; to Frenchmen, it is a *coucou*, to Germans a *Kuckuck*, to Scotsmen, a *gowk*, to Swedes a *gök*, to Poles a *kukulka*, to Spanish speakers a *cuclillo*. In every European language the cuckoo is named for its call, which is actually the spring mating song of the male.

As you can see from the list above, there were many different ways of interpreting the cuckoo's call. The Anglo-Saxons heard it as "gay-ahk," which they wrote *géac*. The Normans brought in the Old French name *cucu*, which became the English name. In Shakespeare's time, "cuckoo" was spelled *cuckow*. Up to about 1800, most people pronounced the *cuck* to rhyme with "duck," but since then it has rhymed with "cook" or with "fluke."

The European cuckoo has earned a very bad name by its practice of laying its eggs in other birds' nests. The cuckoo's egg hatches together with the host bird's eggs, or a little before. The new-hatched cuckoo chick scrunches down in the bottom of the nest and heaves out its nestmates and the unhatched eggs by shoving them with its back.

This seems like truly evil behavior, but the cuckoo chick doesn't even know what it is doing. It is simply following a behavior pattern that was "programmed" into it from before birth. Blind instinct makes it crouch down in the nest, and when baby birds or eggs roll down onto its back and touch the sensitive spots there, another instinctive reflex makes the cuckoo chick push them up and out, just as we instinctively spit bad-tasting things out of our mouths. The mother cuckoo, too, is following an instinctive pattern of behavior that her far-off ancestors evolved hundreds or thousands of years ago. It is not simply that cuckoos are too lazy to build their own nests and rear their own young. They no longer know how.

The host birds, in any case, do not seem to be aware of the deception. As long as the "right" number of eggs are in the nest, they are satisfied. And the female cuckoo has kept the number "right" by destroying one of the host birds' eggs. Another thing: Female cuckoos have an uncanny knack for leaving their eggs with birds whose eggs match the color and markings of their own.

When the eggs hatch, the host birds appear to be happy to feed the cuckoo chick, even though it may soon grow to be much larger than their own. They, too, are driven by instinct. When they see the gaping mouth of a baby bird *in their nest*, they automatically respond by stuffing it with food. Their own young, which the cuckoo has pushed out onto the ground, are ignored because they are not in the right place. Slaves to their instincts, the host birds keep on feeding the cuckoo chick even after it has grown so big that it fills the nest and they have to stand on its back to feed it. Some scientists think that the host birds get extra satisfaction from feeding the cuckoo chick because it has such a wide, gaping mouth, and therefore gives them an extra-powerful signal of "feed me!"

Two species of cuckoos live in North America: the yellow-billed and black-billed cuckoos. Neither of them looks like the European cuckoo, which resembles a small hawk, and American cuckoos do not share their cousins' parasitic habit of laying eggs in other birds nests. In America, this is done by the cowbirds, which belong to the blackbird family. The American cuckoos look more like stretched-out pigeons. They have some unusual relatives. The roadrunner of the Southwest is one. Another is the ani, a tropical bird with black feathers and a grotesque, hooked beak that makes it look like a witch in a storybook.

Most of the world's 127 species of cuckoos live mainly on insects and caterpillars. They are among the few kinds of birds that will touch fuzzy or hairy caterpillars. American cuckoos eat tremendous quantities of tent caterpillars, tussock-moth larvae, and other destructive caterpillars.

Because the European cuckoo does not build a nest, it got a reputation for laziness, which led in turn to accusations of stupidity. As far back as Shakespeare's time, a stupid person was called a cuckoo. In the United States, "cuckoo" took on the slang meaning of "crazy," which it has today. This may have been suggested by the behavior of the mechanical cuckoo in a badly working cuckoo clock.

Cuckoos spend the winter in the warmer parts of the world and come north in spring to mate. This gave them a reputation as heralds of the spring. In parts of Germany, people felt that spring really began the day the first cuckoo was heard, no matter what the calendar said or what the weather was like. In some places, people believed that the cuckoos always returned on the same day.

Many other beliefs and superstitions grew up around the cuckoo. For instance, it was believed to predict rain by its call. In many parts of the world, including the United States, it was called the rain crow. The Swedes believed that if you heard a cuckoo to the north, it meant sorrow, but a cuckoo to the east meant consolation, to the south, death, and to the west, good luck.

In the southeast of England, it was said that a cuckoo flying overhead was an omen of death, and if a cuckoo and a crow lit on the roof of a house where a hawk was already sitting, there would be three deaths. But since no normal cuckoo or crow would risk its life by coming so near a hawk, the theory has probably never had a test.

Young people in many countries used to ask the cuckoo questions about their future. The number of times it called would indicate how long they would live, how many years a girl would have to wait for a husband, and so on. The Danes used to have a saying that the cuckoo never had time to build a nest because it was always kept busy answering people's questions.

DUCK

Duck comes from the Anglo-Saxon name *duce*, which comes in turn from the verb *ducan*, "to dive." Later it was spelled *duk, dukke, doke,* and *douke* before writers and printers settled on the modern spelling.

Strictly speaking, a "duck" is female, and the male is called a "drake." However, this distinction has pretty much gone out of use, at least in the United States, where "drake" is seldom used.

Together with geese and swans, ducks make up the family of birds known as waterfowl. There are too many kinds of ducks to even begin to list them here, but all ducks share certain basic characteristics. They are plump-bodied birds designed for a life in the water. They have a thick layer of fat under their skins, which keeps them warm and makes them slightly buoyant. Special oil glands keep their feathers waterproof; otherwise the weight of waterlogged feathers would drag them down. Ducks' webbed feet spread out to make efficient paddles on the power stroke as they swim and fold up to reduce effort on the recovery stroke. Their short, muscular legs are set far back on their bodies. This gives them an awkward, waddling gait on land but helps them in swimming. Ducks are good fliers, and many of them migrate long distances.

Wild ducks are divided into several groups. The largest is the dipping ducks, which are named for their method of feeding. They tilt up their tails and dip their heads and necks underwater to reach their food, which is mainly water plants, plus small animals such as tadpoles, minnows, crayfish, and insects. The familiar mallard duck is one of the dipping ducks, and most of our domestic breeds of ducks are descended from the dipping ducks.

Another large group of ducks is the diving ducks, which dive down to feed in deeper water than the dipping ducks can reach. Some diving ducks dive quite deep. Some have been caught in fishermen's nets as deep as 100 feet down.

The perching ducks, a rather small group, spend much of their time in forests. They nest in hollow trees, sometimes quite high above the ground. When the ducklings are old enough to leave the nest, they jump down to the ground. They are so light that even a drop of twenty or thirty feet does not hurt them. The beautiful little wood duck is one of the perching ducks. In the fall, flocks of wood ducks sometimes march through the woods feasting on acorns.

There are many other kinds of ducks, but there is not room to describe them here.

Man began to keep ducks perhaps as long as 5,000 years ago. The first people to domesticate the ducks were the Egyptians, who lived along the marshy banks of the Nile River, where there was plenty of water and mud for the ducks to dabble around in. The ancient Chinese also pioneered in raising ducks. The white Pekin duck of China, which is descended from tamed mallards, is one of the major breeds raised today in the United States. Another common domestic breed is the Muscovy duck. Muscovy was an old name for Russia, but the Muscovy duck was named for its musky odor, not because it came from Russia. Its native home is in South America. Muscovy ducks belong to a group of ducks that like to perch in trees, and they sometimes perch on the roof of a house. This can make for a very messy roof.

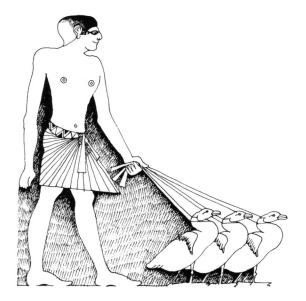

"Duck" as a pet name or term of endearment goes back to the late 1500's. In the late 1800's and early 1900's "ducky" was slang for "attractive," "cute," and "really great." But by the time of World War II it degenerated into pure sarcasm. If someone answered "just ducky" to a question, you knew that things were going all wrong and he was in a foul (not "fowl") humor.

In the mid-1800's London financiers invented the term "lame duck" for a bankrupt stockbroker. Unable to pay his debts, the disgraced broker could only "waddle out of the alley like a lame duck." In the United States "lame duck" came to mean a Congressman or Senator who had been beaten in an election and was limping through the last days of his term. Lame-duck Congressmen and Senators sometimes passed very unpopular bills, knowing that they would not be around to take the heat from the voters when the bills became law. More often they loafed.

A "lame duck" may be crippled, but a "dead duck" is in a really desperate situation. A government official might say, "If the newspapers get hold of what I did with my income tax, I'm a dead duck."

"Duck soup" is an expression meaning "very easy." Scholars have been puzzled by it, because duck soup is no easier to make than chicken soup or turkey soup, and all of them are a chore to prepare. Perhaps it began as "easy as eating duck soup" and was cut down from there.

"To duck," in the sense of ducking down or dodging something, goes back to the 1500's. "Ducking" in the sense of pushing a person down in the water goes back about two centuries earlier. In the 1500's and 1600's an instrument called the ducking stool was used to punish common scolds and other public nuisances. It was a long pole mounted like a seesaw, with a seat on one end in which the offender was fastened. In front of a crowd of jeering neighbors, the offender (usually a woman) was dipped into the village pond or stream one or more times, depending on how much she had aggravated the judge. Sometimes the ducking stool was mounted on wheels so that it could be pulled through the streets, increasing the humiliation of the offender. Ducking stools were used in the New England colonies, but the custom came from Old England, where it lingered long after it had gone out of use in the New World. The last person in England to be sentenced to the ducking stool was a woman named Sarah Leake, in 1819. But she got off easily, because the village pond was almost dry, and the forces of the law had to be content to wheel her around the streets.

EAGLE

For thousands of years the eagle has been called the king of
birds because of its size, strength, and ferocity. It has been a
favorite emblem of kings and military leaders for just as
long. Rome's conquering legions marched to battle behind
the figure of a bronze eagle. Later rulers who liked to think of
themselves as the heirs of the Roman Empire also took the
eagle as their emblem. A double-headed eagle was the emblem of the Habsburg family, which once ruled Austria,
Hungary, Spain, the Netherlands, Czechoslovakia, and large
chunks of Germany, Poland, Yugoslavia, and Italy. The Rus-
sian tsars also had a double-headed eagle as their royal symbol. North American Indian warriors used eagle feathers as

decorations, rather like medals, and they had to earn the right to wear them by bravery in battle. The Aztecs believed that their chief god told them to settle at a place where they would find an eagle perched on a cactus plant, devouring a snake. This became the site of Mexico City, center of the mighty Aztec Empire. The eagle of the Aztecs, together with its snake, is on Mexico's coat of arms today. And the bald eagle is on the Great Seal of the United States and has been a patriotic symbol ever since the birth of the country.

In spite of the eagle's exalted position, "eagle" is not a scientific designation. It is a name popularly given to a number of large, broad-winged hawks, most of which belong to the Buteo family (from which the name of "buzzard" comes). The experts have never agreed on just where the dividing line beyond which a "hawk" is big enough to be called an "eagle" should be drawn. But there are some birds, like the bald eagle and the golden eagle, that everyone agrees are eagles, and there are others that are borderline cases.

In Anglo-Saxon England the name for an eagle was *ern*.

After the Normans conquered England, the French word *aigle* gradually took over, and *ern* is now found only in crossword puzzles. Englishmen often wrote *aigle* as *egle*, and later the spelling was changed again, to *eagle*, probably about a century before Shakespeare's time. The farthest back the name can be traced is the Latin word for the eagle, *aquila*, which probably comes from *aquilus*, meaning "dark-colored." So, to the Romans, the eagle may have been "the dark one."

The Greek name for the eagle was *aetos*, and the ancient Greeks believed that the eagle was sacred to Zeus, the chief of all the gods. Sometimes Zeus changed himself into an eagle and soared around, visiting mortals. Zeus controlled the thunder and lightning and rain, among other things, so the Greeks believed that the eagle could not be struck by lightning. Peasants in ancient Greece, acting on this belief, used to bury eagles' wings in their fields to prevent thunderstorms from destroying the crops. For some reason, it never occurred to them that Zeus might not appreciate having his sacred birds killed.

Many other peoples besides the Greeks believed that the eagle had supernatural powers. More than 1,000 years before the Greeks became civilized, the Sumerians, who lived in the Middle East, worshiped an eagle god. The Hittites, who came storming out of Turkey to conquer most of the Middle East, used a double-headed eagle as a totem. With a head staring in each direction, this magical bird could never be surprised by an enemy sneaking up from behind; so it was a useful luck symbol for a warrior people. Many American Indian tribes believed the eagle was a thunderbird. The thunderbird was sometimes good, sometimes evil (depending on which tribe was telling the story), but he was always one of the most powerful of the Indian gods. The thunder-bird not only controlled the lightning which could burn down a forest and the rain which the crops must have, but could also work powerful magic of all kinds. He often used his power to punish bad people and reward good people. The Pueblo Indians used to kill a young eagle at the beginning of summer so that its spirit could carry their prayers for rain to the gods.

Sometimes the eagle appeared as a messenger of the gods, swooping down from heaven to warn the people of a disaster about to strike them. Sometimes he brought a gift, such as healing herbs. In many fables and folktales an eagle saves someone's life by knocking over a cup of poison he was about to drink, by luring him away from a wall that was about to collapse on him, and in whatever other ways the storyteller could think up.

In addition to appearing on so many rulers' coats of arms, the eagle often appears on coins and bills, such as the dollar bill of the United States. There used to be a ten-dollar gold coin called the eagle, and a twenty-dollar coin called the double eagle. A stingy person used to be described as holding onto his money so tightly that "it made the eagle scream."

Two kinds of eagles are native to North America: the golden eagle and the bald eagle. The golden eagle is named for the golden-brown color of its neck feathers glinting in sunlight; the bald eagle is named for its white head. The golden eagle is found in Europe and Asia, as well as in North America, and the bald eagle has close relatives—called sea eagles—in many parts of the world. The golden eagle was once found over most of North America, but now it is seldom seen outside the mountain regions of the West, and it is pretty scarce even there, thanks partly to ranchers and "sportsmen" who shoot the eagles from airplanes. Many ranchers hate the eagles because they believe the birds kill lambs and poultry. This the eagles occasionally do, but only because ranchers and farmers have wiped out their main natural food supply: prairie dogs, rabbits, and other small "nuisance" animals. Sometimes eagles feed on poisoned animal carcases that have been left out to kill coyotes. They, too, die. But probably the most important reason for the decline of the golden eagle is the wiping out of its natural prey and the destruction of its natural habitat to make room for farms and ranches.

The bald eagle lives near lakes, large rivers, and the seacoast. It is mainly a fish eater, but it is not a great fisherman. Most of its meals come from dead fish that the eagle finds floating on top of the water or scavenges along the beach. Bald eagles also rob ospreys, which are large fish-eating hawks, of their catch. The eagle flies around the osprey, threatening and harassing it until the osprey drops its fish and flees. The eagle catches the fish in midair and flies back to its nest to devour the stolen tidbit. Bald eagles also eat carrion and catch unwary ducks, mice, rabbits, and snakes. Occasionally they kill fawns and lambs that are too young to escape. Despite these unsavory habits, the bald eagle's noble appearance caused it to be chosen as the symbol of the newly created United States, screaming symbolic defiance at the crowned tyrants of Europe.

Once common, the bald eagle today is even scarcer than the golden eagle. One cause is the lack of nesting places. Bald eagles nest in tall trees that give them a good view of the surrounding country, but most of the trees suitable for nesting have been cut down by builders. Without the right kind of place to build in, the eagles do not build nests, and without nests there are no eggs and no young eagles. But the chief cause of the bald eagle's disappearance is DDT, the wonder chemical that people once thought would solve many of the world's problems by killing harmful insects. DDT is a powerful poison indeed, and kills mosquitoes, flies, and crop-devouring insects very effectively—until the insects develop an immunity to it. The trouble is that DDT does not break down after it has done its job of killing bugs. It stays poisonous indefinitely. Rain, melting snow, and garden sprinklers wash the DDT into the soil and from there into rivers, lakes, and the ocean. Tiny organisms that live in the water absorb DDT into their bodies. When larger creatures eat them, they take on the load of DDT from their victims. But living organisms cannot get rid of DDT. The poisonous chemical stays in their bodies, slowly building up as they take in more. Fish build up a great deal of DDT in this way, and the bald eagle lives mainly on fish.

Bald eagles do not eat enough DDT to kill them, as far as is known, but enough accumulates in their bodies to make things go badly wrong with their reproductive systems. They lay eggs that are sterile and can never hatch, eggs that have shells so weak that they crack when the parent bird sits on them, and eggs with no shells at all. So very few new bald eagles are being produced to replace the old ones that die.

The bald eagle is not the only bird to be affected by DDT. Ospreys have been badly diminished in the same way. Many small birds, such as robins, have been killed outright by eating earthworms containing DDT. It would be a sad thing if our efforts to make the world more comfortable were to end by depriving us of birds, which are so important in the balance of nature and give us pleasure in so many ways.

FINCH

About 25,000,000 to 30,000,000 years ago, grasses and related plants appeared and spread rapidly over the earth. This had all kinds of effects on the evolution of life. As far as birds were concerned, its greatest effect was to cause a whole new group of birds to evolve—birds that were able to take advantage of the vast new food supply provided by the seeds of the grasses. They were (and still are) small to medium-sized birds with short, stout, cone-shaped bills, admirably adapted to serve as built-in seed crackers.

The seed-eating birds flourished and spread over most of the world, splitting up into a dizzying array of species. Scientists today reckon about 700 species in the two families of seed eaters. The scientific names of these families are Fringillidae and Ploceidae. Laymen call them sparrows, finches, and buntings. Actually, the names are used very loosely, so that the same bird may be called a finch and a sparrow or bunting in different countries.

"Finch" itself is a very old name, which scholars have traced back to an ancient Germanic root something like *finkiz*. It sounds as if the name were an imitation of the bird's chirping. The English name "finch" comes directly from the Anglo-Saxon word *finc* (in Anglo-Saxon spelling, *c* was often used to stand for the sound *ch.*) In other languages it took slightly different forms; *Fink* in German, *fink* with a small *f* in Swedish and Norwegian, *vink* in Dutch. In French it is *pinson* and in Spanish *pinzón*, which also happened to be the family name of two of Columbus' ship captains in 1492. Columbus' own name (Colombo in Italian) meant "dove," so one might say that birds were well represented among the leaders.

The Romans used to keep finches in cages, particularly the kind known as the bullfinch, which could be trained to sing like a canary. In Europe and Asia, bullfinches are still popular as cage birds. Canaries themselves are finches.

Scientists classify about 300 kinds of birds as finches of one kind or another, so it is impossible to list all the kinds found in North America. But the goldfinch (sometimes called the wild canary) is the state bird of Iowa and New Jersey; the willow finch, of Washington State; and the purple finch, of New Hampshire. One of the commonest birds around our big cities, the English sparrow, is a finch, too.

On the Galápagos Islands lives a very special group of finches. Cut off from the mainland for thousands of years, the finches evolved into very different species, each one specialized for taking advantage of a different kind of food or a different way of life. One had even learned to use a cactus thorn to dig insect grubs out of wood. Nearly 150 years ago a young English scientist named Charles Darwin spent some time in the Galápagos Islands and studied the finches, along with other animals and plants. The results of his studies helped him work out his famous theory of evolution.

"Finch" is a fairly ordinary family name among people of English descent, as is "Fink" among people of German descent. One of the early heroes of American folklore was a rip-roaring frontiersman named Mike Fink. The Pennsylvania Dutch, whose ancestors came from Germany in the early 1700's, have a legendary bird of happiness called the *Distelfink*, or "thistle finch."

In the late 1800's "fink" took on a new meaning. Workmen were struggling to gain the right to form labor unions. The battle between workers and bosses was fierce and bitter. The employers fought back with every weapon they had, including laws that favored them, private armies to break strikes, and spies to report union organizers to the bosses to be dealt with. German immigrants were prominent in the labor movement, and they called the spies finks, because they "sang" to the bosses like a caged finch bird. "Fink" kept its meaning of a spy or informer for many years, until in the 1960's it was taken up by celebrities as a new "in" word. As an "in" word it soon lost all meaning, so that "fink" is now just a name to call someone you don't like.

FLICKER

The flicker's name comes from its call, flick-flick-flick! It could just as well have come from the bird's flickering, uneven flight, bobbing up and down in the air like a woodpecker. In fact, flickers are woodpeckers, but they seem to be in the process of changing over from life in the trees to life on the ground. Although they still chisel out nest holes in trees, they spend most of their time hopping around on the ground searching for ants, their favorite food. Flickers also eat berries and other fruits, ant eggs and larvae, any insects they can catch, and even spiders.

Flickers can be found (at the right time of the year) all the way from Alaska to the pampas of Argentina. Three species live in North America. The most common is the yellow-shafted flicker, named for the bright-yellow feathers on the undersides of its wings and tail. It can be found all year round in the United States east of the Rocky Mountains, and its summer range spreads into Alaska and much of Canada. West of the Rockies lives the red-shafted flicker, which has red color patches instead of yellow. In the far Southwest lives the gilded flicker, which nests in giant saguaro cactuses.

Some industrious person once counted up 132 folk names for the yellow-shafted flicker. The commonest of them is "yellowhammer." Under this name it is the state bird of Alabama. The name of "yellowhammer" originally belonged to several different small birds in England. The "hammer" part had nothing to do with a woodpecker's hammering at a tree trunk. It actually came from *amore*, an Anglo-Saxon name for small birds. In England nowadays, a "yellowhammer" is most often a yellow bunting.

In parts of Europe, uneducated people used to believe that the yellowhammer was in league with the devil. This superstition must have been left behind when early settlers crossed the Atlantic, for there is no such belief about the American yellowhammer, which is a very different bird in any case.

Adult male flickers have a mustachelike stripe on each side of their bills, black for the yellow-shafted flicker and red for the other two kinds. The mustache is the recognition mark that lets the birds know instantly which sex another flicker belongs to, for females do not have them. During the courting and nesting season, a male flicker will chase away any other male that comes onto his territory, for the mustaches signal "Rival!" Females and immature males lacking mustaches, do not count as rivals, and they are not attacked.

A scientist once did an experiment with a mated pair of flickers. While the male was away, he glued false mustaches on the female. When the male returned, he mistook his mate for another male and attacked her viciously. The female, bewildered by his sudden change of behavior, fled in confusion. Back and forth across the nesting territory went the furious chase, until finally the female spotted a culvert where she hid. The scientist then removed the false mustaches from the exhausted female, and the male welcomed her back to the nest as if nothing had happened. It was a striking demonstration of how powerfully birds are governed by their instincts, though unscientific people might say it merely showed that birds are really "bird-brained."

GOOSE

Goose comes from the Anglo-Saxon name *gos*, which came from an old Teutonic word, *gans*. The original root from which it came was probably an imitation of a goose's honking. *Gos* had a long *o* like *go*. In the Middle Ages the *o* was doubled to show that it was long. Then pronunciations changed, and "goose" rhymed with "loose" and "moose."

A male goose is called a gander, and baby geese are called goslings. "Gander" may have been an old Germanic form of "goose-he," and "gosling" is just *gos* with the diminutive ending *ling* tacked on. "Geese," the plural form, is a living fossil of a word. It is a relic from the time when many words changed the vowel sound inside them to become plural instead of adding s at the end. Very few such words are left in English "Mouse-mice" and "foot-feet" are certainly the only ones we hear ordinarily.

Geese are related to the swans and ducks, and they are about halfway between them in size. (However, some geese are so small that they are called ducks, and some ducks are so large that they are called geese.) Geese have longer necks than ducks, though not as long as swans. They are vegetarians and spend a lot of time on land nibbling on grass, roots, and green leaves. They are much better walkers than ducks since their legs are set farther forward on their bodies, but by the same token, they are not as good swimmers.

The most numerous and the best-known wild goose of North America is the Canada goose, which reaches a body length of two feet and a wingspread of five and one half feet or more. There are at least ten subspecies of the Canada goose, all of different sizes, which makes things pretty confusing for the bird-watcher.

Another common wild goose is the brant, which looks like a smallish Canada goose except that it does not have white cheek patches, as its larger cousin does.

One of the most beautiful of all geese is the white snow goose, which breeds in the far north of Canada and Alaska. The sight of a flock of migrating snow geese is something never to be forgotten. The blue goose (actually more gray than blue) is a dark form of the snow goose.

The rarest goose in the world is the nene, a small goose native to the Hawaiian Islands. Never very numerous, the nenes were killed off by man, who hunted the adults, and his pigs and dogs, which raided the nests and devoured eggs and goslings. Mongooses, brought in by sugar planters in the

1800's to keep down rats, also took a toll of the defenseless nenes. By 1950 only thirty wild nenes were left, plus a few in zoos. The nene is now protected by law, and the wild birds are making a slow comeback in Hawaii Volcanoes National Park. More nenes live in protected flocks supported by conservation groups in other parts of the world. The nene is the state bird of Hawaii.

All the American wild geese except the nene breed in the far north and come south when the Arctic winter cuts off their food supplies. But some Canada geese, attracted by people who feed them, now stay the year round in the Northern states, raising their families in suburban parks and private ponds.

The ancestor of domestic geese is the big wild graylag of northern Europe and Asia. In many parts of Europe, geese were one of the major domestic animals. People kept huge herds of them, and they were driven out to pasture every day by a gooseherd—usually a small boy or girl—who whacked them with a long stick to keep them from straying away.

The goose was truly an animal of many uses. One of the chief ones was producing feathers. Quilts stuffed with goose feathers were standard equipment in central European houses before central heating came into use, and they are still popular. Anybody who has slept under a goose-feather quilt can testify that they are very warm, although they have an annoying habit of falling off the bed in the middle of the night. Goose feathers, trimmed into pens, were the standard writing instrument before the steel-tipped pen was invented in the early 1800's. When properly trimmed, goose quills write well, but they wear out quickly and have to be resharpened about as often as a lead pencil. The little knife we call a penknife was designed especially for trimming quill pens.

Roast goose was a favorite dish in many European countries. Traditionally, goose was eaten in the fall, when the birds were fat and their meat was rich and juicy. St. Michael's Day, or Michaelmas, and St. Martin's Day were the days of the great goose feasts. But the goose's usefulness did not end here. Goose eggs were also eaten. And every roasted goose yielded large amounts of pure white fat that was used for cooking.

Man's first tame geese were probably kept as sacred birds, perhaps as long as 5,000 years ago. In some ancient religions, geese were symbols of fertility. They were also symbols of marital fidelity, for wild geese normally mate for life. The Romans kept a flock of sacred geese at the Temple of Juno, inside the city of Rome. Legend says that in 390 B.C. enemy raiders tried to infiltrate the city by night, when all good Romans were sleeping. The sacred geese saved the city by raising an alarm. There could be some truth to this legend, for geese are suspicious of strangers and make good watchdogs.

Despite this, geese have a reputation for stupidity, though as birds go, they are not particularly stupid. Wild geese are

alert, wary birds. Tame geese, being protected by man, have little need for intelligence, so whatever they have probably lies unused. At any rate, to call a person a goose is no compliment to his brainpower.

When we are cold or frightened, tiny lumps stand out on our skins. We call these gooseflesh, goose bumps, or goose pimples from their resemblance to the tiny bumps on the skin of a plucked goose.

Before the end of World War II, soldiers in the German Army paraded with a peculiar step. It was named the goosestep by Englishmen who thought it looked like the stiff-legged waddle of a goose. The goosestep is performed by lifting each leg straight out in front of you without bending the knee. The goosestep became a symbol of dictatorships, and it is still used in the armies of some nations ruled by dictators.

"He's cooked his own goose" means "he's really got himself into trouble." "I'll cook his goose for him" means "I'll fix him." "His goose is cooked" means "he's done for." Where these culinary metaphors came from is hard to say, but they are expressive.

"Killing the goose that laid the golden eggs" comes from an old Greek fable about a greedy king. This king owned a magical goose that laid eggs of purest gold. Impatient at getting only one or two golden eggs a day, the king killed the goose and cut it open, hoping to get control of the whole golden-egg supply at once. Of course, he got no more eggs. So "to kill the goose that laid the golden eggs" came to mean doing yourself out of something good through your own greed and stupidity.

One of the strangest beliefs about geese was that a certain species developed from barnacles, little sea animals that live on rocks, pilings, ships, whales, and floating wood. This curious belief must have developed from the fact that one kind of barnacle, the goose barnacle, does look strangely like a tiny goose fastened to a timber by its head. The "neck" is actually a stalk that anchors the barnacle to its support. The barnacle's shell is shaped somewhat like the plump body of a goose. From the open end of the shell protrude a group of little feathery organs that could suggest real feathers. Actually, they are feet with which the barnacle traps floating food particles. The myth of the barnacle goose lasted into the 1700's. It was particularly strong in the Middle Ages, when men liked to believe in miracles and when good Catholics insisted that the goose was really a "fish" so that they could eat it on Fridays and during Lent, when meat was forbidden. The barnacle goose (a real goose, by the way) sometimes visits the east coast of North America in the fall.

A famous scientist named Konrad Lorenz did many experiments with geese to learn about the laws of animal behavior. In trying to discover how newly hatched goslings learn to recognize their mother, he found that the first moving object they saw was "imprinted" on their brains as their mother. Normally this worked without a hitch, since their mother would naturally be the first thing they saw. But Lorenz took some goose eggs away from the mother and hatched them in an incubator. He stood watch at hatching time so that he would be the first moving object the goslings saw. As he had suspected, they adopted him as their mother and tried to follow him everywhere. The kindhearted scientist raised his little goslings to maturity. While they were small, he had to squat down so that they could see him and waddle along uncomfortably, gabbling to them in a soothing tone. As Lorenz said later, it was the first time a man was ever mother to a goose.

Thinking of mothers and geese, what about the Mother Goose rhymes? Was there ever a real Mother Goose? And did she make up the rhymes herself, or did she memorize a vast number of traditional rhymes that someone else wrote down? Some Boston people used to insist that there was a real Mother Goose, the wife of an early Boston settler named Isaac Goose. According to this story, Mother Goose (whose actual name was Elizabeth) used to recite old rhymes to her children until they had heard them so often they couldn't forget them if they wanted to. Later Mother Goose moved in with one of her married daughters and recited the rhymes to her grandchildren until her son-in-law was ready to climb the walls. In revenge, he copied down the most ridiculous of them and published them in 1719. But no copy of this book of rhymes has ever been found, making the story rather suspicious. Besides, a Frenchman named Charles Perrault had published a book of children's tales called *Tales of My Mother the Goose* twenty-three years earlier, which pretty much knocks holes in the Boston theory.

Perrault's tales were old favorites, and he picked a name out of French folklore for his title. The name of "Mother Goose" probably came from a Queen of France who lived nearly 1,000 years earlier, Bertha Goosefoot, the mother of Charlemagne. Scholars think she was nicknamed for her big, floppy feet. After Bertha died, French peasants told stories about her and transformed her into a legendary heroine, a good-natured mother who was always telling stories to her big family of children to keep them quiet while she was busy spinning.

GRACKLE

The Romans had a word for it: *graculus*. This was the name
they gave to the jackdaw, that noisy, thievish little cousin of
the crow, probably in imitation of the birds' rackety chattering. In time the Latin name *graculus* and its English form,
"grackle," came to be applied loosely to many different kinds
of noisy, chattering birds, including some starlings and the
famous talking mynas of India. In America the name of
"grackle" was handed on to a medium-sized bird with beautiful, iridescent feathers that change from black to blue,
green, purple, or bronze as the angle of the light changes.

The American grackles are most closely related to black-birds and cowbirds, and they often flock together with them. Like blackbirds, grackles are very sociable birds, and they often join together in huge flocks numbering thousands of birds. Such large flocks are bound to do a great deal of nuisance, if only by the messes they make on streets, buildings, and cars. In the spring of 1974 a flock of grackles, black-birds, and starlings descended on the region around Washington, D.C. The number of birds was estimated at 10,000,000. Local authorities annoyed the birds with whistles, sirens, flashing lights, and recordings of the birds' own alarm calls to drive them away. They even fired propane-powered cannons. Nothing worked.

Grackles will eat almost anything: insects, seeds, fruits, frogs, and any reptiles small enough for them to overpower. Some grackles even learn to catch small fish. Unfortunately, grackles also have the unpleasant habit of eating the eggs and young of other birds. They make up for this to some extent by eating harmful insects.

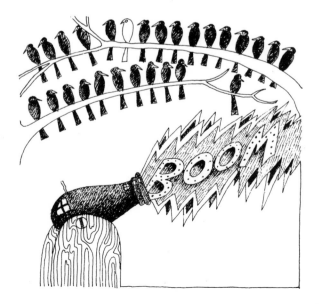

GULL

The gull's name was probably inspired by its plaintive, wailing call. Language scholars believe that "gull" is an English version of the bird's name in Welsh—*gwylan*—or in Cornish —*guilan*. Both these names probably came from an old Celtic root meaning "wailing." The English picked up the Celtic name from their Welsh or Cornish neighbors some time in the 1300's. Before then, they used the old Anglo-Saxon name for the gull, *mew*, again referring to the mournful, mewing cry of the bird. The Anglo-Saxons often called gulls sea-mews to make it perfectly clear to their listeners that they were not talking about kittens, which, as is well known, also say "mew."

Although most people think of gulls as seabirds and usually call them sea gulls, they are actually shorebirds and seldom venture far from land. They also live far inland, on lakes, reservoirs, large rivers, and marshlands.

Gulls are not fussy eaters. They eat fish, shellfish, and carrion. Long ago, they learned how to crack open the hard shells of clams and snails by dropping them on a rock from high up in the air; nowadays the birds also make use of man's paved streets and highways. At many a shore resort, streets and parking lots near the water are littered with the remains of the gulls' shellfish snacks. Usually the birds do their shellfish cracking very early in the morning, before traffic gets in their way.

Gulls have benefited from man in another way. Man's garbage is an immense free lunch for gulls. This is why gulls hang around harbors and follow ships several miles out to sea. Many city garbage dumps are patrolled by white-winged armies of greedy gulls, which rise in a fluttering cloud when a truck comes to dump a new load of goodies and settle down to feast again as soon as the disturbance has passed. As a matter of fact, gulls will eat just about anything they can get, including the eggs and young of other birds and even the eggs and chicks of their neighbor gulls at the nesting grounds.

But the nesting grounds are not scenes of horrid cannibalistic orgies. When the gulls are not disturbed by predators or other intruders (such as curious human visitors), they are like crowded but orderly cities. Each pair of gulls has a small territory that the male has staked out at the beginning of the breeding season. The gulls patrol this territory jealously, driving out any gulls that trespass on it. This is done with very little actual fighting, because over thousands of years the gulls have developed an intricate code of behavior. One might say that they are programmed to respect each other's territories once they are established. (This respect only operates when there is a gull in the territory to defend it, but even that is something.)

A nesting ground may contain hundreds or even thousands of gulls. In order for the gulls to get along with a minimum of battle and bloodshed, they have evolved a regular signal code along with their behavior rituals. They communicate with each other by calls and gestures. Chicks have a special call for help and food. Parent gulls have calls for warning their chicks of danger, for signaling "all clear," and warning intruders off their territories. To threaten an intruder on his territory, a male gull may rear up with his head cocked back to deliver a punishing peck, his wings brought forward, ready to deliver a lightning punch with the knuckle, and his eyes squinting meanly. A female or a young gull will signal "I'm OK—I mean no harm" by crouching down close to the ground with its head stretched forward. In this position it cannot deliver a peck, and the angry gull recognizes this and does not attack. A hungry gull chick pecks at the tip of its father's or mother's bill to signal that it wants to be fed. A red spot on the parent's bill tells the chick where to peck. The parent responds to this signal by regurgitating partly digested food for the chick. A Dutch scientist named Niko Tinbergen, who has spent his life studying gulls, has discovered many other gull signals.

Gulls once played an important part in the history of the West. In 1848, Mormon settlers in Utah planted their grain and watched patiently while the young sprouts came up. This grain would feed them while they built their desert commonwealth, far from the enemies who had driven them from their homes and farms back East. To their horror, huge swarms of crickets appeared and began to devour every growing thing in sight. If the crickets ate their grain crops, the Mormons faced disaster. They gathered in their temple and prayed for help. Suddenly, flocks of gulls appeared and ate up the crickets. Enough of the crop was saved to keep the settlers fed through the winter. Ever since then Mormons have honored the gull, and in Salt Lake City there is a famous statue of two gulls commemorating the time the gulls rescued the Mormons. The gull is the state bird of Utah.

In English there is a word, "gullible," meaning "easily fooled." This expression was not invented because of the gull's stupidity, for gulls are actually rather crafty birds. Apparently it came from the lingo of seventeenth-century cardsharps and confidence men. These practitioners of chicanery once called their victims pigeons and referred to their various methods of cheating them as "plucking the pigeon." When the "pigeons" began to understand what this thieves' lingo meant, the con men changed the expression to "grope the gull." From this came related expressions such as "to gull" (to trick) someone and "gullible."

HAWK

Hawk comes from the Anglo-Saxon name *heafoc*, which comes from an old Teutonic root meaning "to seize." So "hawk" originally meant a bird that seizes its prey, as many hawks do, killing it by piercing its vital organs with their long, sharp talons. Other hawks swoop down on their prey with terrific speed and deliver a back-breaking punch with their talons clenched.

Hawks and their relatives the eagles and vultures all have sharp, hooked bills for tearing off mouthfuls of flesh and powerful talons for holding the prey and carrying it off to the nest to eat. All of them hunt by sight, and they have remarkably keen eyes. For hundreds of years sharp-sighted, vigilant people have been called hawk-eyed or eagle-eyed. Scientists have examined hawks' eyes and found that they were about eight times as powerful as human eyes. This is why hawks can spot a small animal like a rabbit in a field from hundreds of feet up in the air.

Long ago, man learned how to train hawks for hunting birds and small animals. Ever since then hawking has been a sport of the aristocracy from Japan to Ireland and from Norway to North Africa. At some periods it has been very popular, but nowadays only a few enthusiasts carry it on. One reason is the expense and time it takes to train a hawk. Another may be the growing scarcity of game as more and more of the world gets paved over and built on. A third is the slow growth of the idea that animals should be treated kindly, for hawking is a cruel sport.

The hawks most used in hunting were the falcons, a family of hawks with long, pointed wings and beaks with a tooth or notch in the upper bill. In fact, they were used so much more than other breeds of hawks that the sport as a whole was usually called falconry. Different species of falcons were used for hunting different sizes of game. The big, powerful gyrfalcon could kill birds as large as cranes and storks. The medium-sized peregrine falcon (known in the United States as the duck hawk) was used on waterfowl, pheasants, rabbits, and the like. The small merlins and sparrow hawks were used for pigeons and songbirds.

The falcon's name comes from *faucon*, a French form of the Latin name *falco*, which comes from *falx, falcis*, meaning "sickle," from the curved, sicklelike shape of the falcon's powerful talons. The gyrfalcon (pronounced JER-falcon) carries in its name an old German word, *giri*, meaning "greedy." So it is really the "greedy falcon." The peregrine

76

falcon's name comes from the Latin word for a foreigner or a traveler, *peregrinus*. It may have been given this name because people of the Middle Ages thought it had no real home, but wandered about constantly looking for prey, or possibly because young birds to be trained for hunting were captured on their flight away from the breeding grounds to the winter feeding grounds. Other hawks were usually taken from their nest before they could fly, but the peregrine's nest was hard to find and harder yet to get at. An old name for the peregrine was the gentle falcon, which seems like an odd name for such a savage predator. But in this case "gentle" did not mean that the peregrine had a soft, tender disposition. It meant "belonging to the nobility" (the original meaning of "gentle"), for in medieval Europe only noblemen were allowed to hunt with peregrine falcons.

In fact, there was a strict system under which different hawks were allotted to persons of different ranks. Only a king could have a gyrfalcon. Peregrine falcons were limited to nobles of the rank of earl or higher. A plain knight had to be content with a smaller breed of falcon called a sacre. Ladies could have the still smaller merlin. A young man of the privileged classes could have a hobby, which was a small hawk that was not considered a very good hunter. A yeoman —that is, a common man who owned his own land, which was rather uncommon in the Middle Ages—could hawk with a goshawk, whose name means "goose-hawk." The goshawk could kill birds as big as a goose, but it was a slower flier than the falcons; so the nobility did not consider it worth keeping for themselves. It was, of course, quite good enough for a lowborn commoner. In one set of rules, a "poor man" was permitted to have a tiercel (male) goshawk. The reason was probably that among hawks the males are smaller and less powerful than the females. A priest's allotted hawk was the tiny sparrow hawk, which normally lives on insects. A knave, or servant, was allowed only a kestrel, a small hawk that was considered absolutely useless. An emperor was allotted the eagle (probably only to be paraded around on a perch on important occasions, for eagles are very different to train) and, for some obscure reason, the vulture, which doesn't hunt, but can't be beaten at finding dead animals.

Since falconry was a sport for privileged people, an incredibly complicated jargon grew up around it. To master this jargon, you had to have grown up among people who used it all the time. A person who had not been brought up as an aristocrat, even though he might have been promoted to the aristocracy for some useful service to the king, would be sure to make mistakes and give away his humble origin. Like other specialized jargons, it was an effective way of putting down outsiders.

Since hawks had such high status (among humans) and were known for their keen sight, they acquired a rather undeserved reputation for intelligence. Authors of old-time detective stories used to describe their detective heroes as "hawk-faced" to make readers think of them as keen and intelligent. A famous humorist once complained about this habit of making detectives hawk-faced. As he pointed out, the hawk is a rather stupid bird, while the chimpanzee ranks next to man in intelligence. Therefore, he said, authors should give the detective a face like a chimpanzee, and the crime would be solved in no time flat.

HERON

The herons are a family of long-necked, long-legged wading birds with long, spearlike bills. They are often confused with storks and cranes, although they are related only distantly to the storks and not at all to the cranes and could not interbreed with them even if they wanted to. Of course, they would not want to, for the courtship rituals and signals of these birds are so different that whatever excited one of them would have no meaning at all for the other two.

Ancient German tribesmen called the heron a *Heiger*. When German warriors conquered France in the 400's, their French subjects turned it into *hairon*. The Normans brought *hairon* to England, and our modern word "heron" is not very different from it. An old form of "heron" was *hern,* which is no longer used except by poets desperate for a rhyme or trying to create an archaic effect.

Medieval Frenchmen called a young heron a *heronceau,* and Englishmen who tried to copy them corrupted it into *hernshaw.* All the old names for the heron probably come from an ancient Indo-European root meaning "to utter sharp cries," which would refer to the loud alarm squawks of the birds.

The heron family includes the bitterns and egrets, but here we shall cover only those birds which are called herons. All the herons are specialized for life in marshlands and shallow water, where they hunt fish, frogs, crayfish, and other small water creatures. The great blue heron, one of the largest American species, sometimes flies inland to hunt mice and gophers.

Different species of herons have different techniques of fishing. Some of the smaller herons perch just above the water and wait for a fish to swim by. Others wade out after the fish. Some spread their wings to make a shadow on the water. Small fish swim to this cool, shaded spot, where the heron catches and eats them. Still others do a kind of shuffling dance in the water to stir up fish from the bottom.

The longer a heron's legs, the deeper the water it feeds in. This keeps the different species from crowding each other and avoids putting too much strain on the food supply at any one spot.

The largest heron of North America is the great white heron, which stands four to five feet tall and has a wingspread of nearly six feet. Almost as big is the great blue, a much more widespread and abundant bird. The small green heron, which is really more gray or blue than green, lives along wooded streams and ponds. When alarmed, it flies off awkwardly with loud calls of "Skeeow!" Another common heron is the black-crowned night heron, a short-legged bird that hunts mostly at night. New Englanders call it the quawk or qua-bird from its cry.

Herons were once hunted in Europe or Asia, usually with the aid of falcons. Hunters praised the courage of the falcon in overcoming the much larger heron. But in reality it was no contest at all. On the ground, the heron would have been more than a match for the falcon, but in the air it was defenseless against the killer that clung to its back, out of reach, piercing its vitals with merciless talons.

Herons were a popular dish at medieval banquets, and knights used to compete in making foolhardy vows to perform deeds of bravery when the heron was carried in. Over the roasted corpse of the heron, one drunken knight would swear to wear a patch over one eye until he had killed six men in battle for his liege lord. Another would top this by vowing to sleep in his armor until he had fought ten of the bravest champions of Christendom for the honor of his lady love, and so on. Many of them must have been sorry the next morning when spiteful rivals reminded them of the tasks they had taken on.

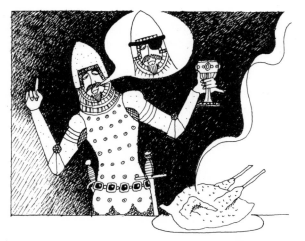

JUNCO

One of the most familiar winter visitors to the bird feeder is the cheery little slate-colored junco, a plump, sparrow-sized bird that hardly seems to notice the cold as long as it can find something to eat.

Junco is the Spanish word for "reed." Reasonably enough, it was one of the names given to the European reed bunting, a small bird that nests in reed-filled swamps. For some inexplicable reason, around 1830 it was given to a small, dark-colored American bird of the finch family that lives in pine and spruce forests. Up to the early 1900's it was mainly the scientists who used the name "junco" so loosely. Most people called them "snowbirds" because when they came south from their summer nesting grounds in Canada, winter was never far behind. Other popular names were black snowbird, whitebill, and black chipping bird. But now "junco" is firmly established.

KINGFISHER

Kingfisher comes from *king* plus *fisher*. The name, which dates from the early 1400's, well suits the bold little bird that fishes for its living. Kingfishers like to perch on an overhanging branch above a lake or stream, watching the water intently. When they spot a small fish, they dive headfirst, seizing it in their strong, sharp-edged beaks and carrying it back to their perch to eat. Kingfishers also eat crayfish, frogs, snakes, lizards, and water insects.

The belted kingfisher, the only American species north of the Mexican border zone, is a dull blue-gray with a white underside. The female has a chestnut stripe across her breast, adding a touch of color to her drab plumage. But most of the world's kingfishers are beautifully colored in bright greens and blues, often with contrasting patches of red or white. A medieval European legend relates that the kingfisher was once a dull, gray creature. But when Noah let it out of the Ark, it flew straight toward the setting sun. The heat of the sun burned its breast to a rich red-brown, and its back took on the color of the evening sky.

Kingfishers are distantly related to the crows and jays, and they are spread over most of the world. The largest of the kingfishers is the kookaburra, which lives in Australia. It is also known as the laughing jackass, from its loud, braying call, which sounds oddly like the laughter of a madman. Kookaburras utter this call at dawn and again at sunset, when they go to roost. Kookaburras may live quite far from water. They eat snakes and lizards, varied with an occasional snack of young birds.

When ponds and streams freeze over in wintertime, kingfishers may move to the seashore to find open water where they can catch fish. The ancient Greeks noticed this habit and believed that the birds bred on the sea in a floating nest (actually, they dig deep burrows in stream banks and nest

there). The poetic Greeks spun fact and fancy into a legend about Alcyone, daughter of Boreas, the god of the North Wind. Alcyone fell in love with Ceyx, son of the Morning Star, and they were married. The young couple were very happy together, so happy that they roused the jealousy of Zeus, who punished them by raising a storm at sea and drowning Ceyx. His ghost appeared to Alcyone and told her the story. Grief-stricken, she threw herself into the sea and also perished. In pity, the other gods turned both Alcyone and Ceyx into kingfishers and decreed that the seas should be calm and the sun shine for seven days before and seven days after the shortest day of the year. During this time, the Greeks said, the kingfishers built their nests and hatched their young. The sea around Greece is usually quiet around this time, helping bolster the legend. The Greeks and the Romans, who picked up many beliefs from the Greeks, called this period of calm and peace the "halcyon days." (Halcyon is the Latin form of Alcyone.) Ever since then, periods of peace and prosperity have been called halcyon days.

Europeans had other legends about the kingfisher. They believed that the dried body of a kingfisher would ward off thunderbolts. If it were hung in a clothes closet, it would keep moths away. If a dried kingfisher were hung by a string from the ceiling of a room, its bill would point to the direction the wind was coming from.

None of these superstitions seems to have stuck to the American kingfisher, which goes its carefree way without the threat of being turned into a lightning protector, mothball, or weather vane.

LOON

An Indian legend tells that the loon was not always a bird.
Long ago two men went out together to fish. One had good
luck and soon caught a whole canoeful of fish. The other
caught nothing. Filled with envious hatred, he knocked his
friend on the head, stole his fish, and cut out his tongue so
that he couldn't report the crime. When the poor Indian
regained consciousness and managed to get to shore, he
could not talk. He could only wail. So the Great Spirit transformed him into a loon and turned the evildoer into a crow.
Ever since then, when you hear a loon calling, it is the spirit
of the wronged fisherman pleading for justice.

The Indians of the Northland had many tales about the loon. But the name "loon" itself comes from the Norsemen, not the Indians, for loons are found in northern Europe and Asia, as well as the northern United States and Canada.

When Norse invaders settled in the north of Britain 1,100 years ago, they found many of the same birds they had known in their homeland. One of these was a large water bird with striking black-and-white markings on its wings and back, which could swim and dive like a seal. The Norse name for this bird was *lomr* (pronounced LOOM-er), a name they used for several diving birds. In time, *lomr* became *loom*, which was much easier to pronounce. In the early 1600's it became "loon" with an *n*. Why this last change happened we do not know. It may have been because there was already a "loon" in the English language, a name which carried the meanings of "rogue" or "clumsy, oafish lout." Fishermen may have called the birds rogues because they eat fish that the men want to catch and sometimes tear holes in the fishermen's nets. Anyone might have called loons clumsy and oafish on land, for their legs are set so far back on their long, heavy bodies that it is all they can do to keep from falling on their faces as they awkwardly shuffle along. The fact that their legs are buried inside their bodies up to the ankle joint does not make walking any easier.

But in the water the loons have few equals as swimmers. The peculiar leg design that cripples them on land gives them an extraordinarily powerful kick, and they scoot along like a diver with swim fins, using their strong, stubby wings for steering and balancing. Most birds have hollow bones to make them as light as possible. Loons have heavy, solid bones that make their bodies nearly as dense as water. By emptying their lungs and squeezing trapped air from under their feathers, they become heavy enough to sink right down, a great advantage when chasing fish or escaping from enemies. At the same time, their special body chemistry lets them store enough oxygen for a whole minute of underwater action. When fleeing from enemies, loons can swim underwater as long as five minutes, though this is not something they can keep up for very long. Because of their superb skill in diving, the British call them divers or great northern divers. Loons can dive very deep—one was trapped in a fishing net 240 feet down—though they usually catch their prey in much shallower water. Loons are so completely adapted for life in the water that they almost never come to land except to nest.

Loons cannot take off from land and even have trouble getting airborne from the water, but once they are in the air they are strong fliers. Some have been clocked at 60 miles per hour.

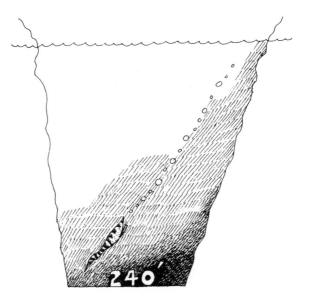

There are four species of loons, and among them they cover the northern fringe of the world. Three species are known in North America: the three-foot common loon and the two-foot red-throated and arctic loons. The loons spend their summers in far northern lakes, where they nest and feed, and their winters along warm southern seashores.

Loons are very talkative birds, and they have a large repertory of calls. One is a long, wailing cry, rather like the mournful howl of a wolf, which to many people symbolizes the spirit of the wild North Woods. Another is an eerie cachinnation that sounds like the sinister laughter of a maniac. It was probably this bloodcurdling laugh that gave rise to the expression "crazy as a loon." It may also be a parent of "loony"—slang for "crazy"—along with "lunatic," which comes from *luna*, the Latin word for "moon," and originally meant someone who had been rendered insane by the light of the moon falling on him. Star watchers, don't worry! It was an ancient superstition with no basis in fact.

People in ancient times had plenty of superstitions about loons. The Norwegians used to believe that the call of a loon meant that someone was going to be drowned. Northern Europeans and American Indians believed that the call of the loon meant that rain would come or even caused the rain. Many northern Indian tribes had legends about how the loon dived to the bottom of the sea and brought up mud, from which the Great Spirit created the land. The Algonquin Indians believed that loons were the messengers of the superhuman hero Glooskap. In northern Europe and Siberia, people believed that when loons took to the air, they were escorting the soul of a dead person to heaven. There were many similar beliefs—and in some places people considered loons sacred. Not bad for a clumsy, oafish, fish-stealing bird that can hardly walk without falling on its face!

MAGPIE

The magpie is a smaller cousin of the crows, with a long tail and striking black-and-white plumage, set off by green on the tail and a blue wing patch. It is notorious for its noisy chattering and its thievish habits—magpies will pick up any bright objects they can lift and carry them off to their nests, where they hoard them.

The Romans called the magpie *pica*. In Old French this became *pie*. The Normans took this name with them to England (not the bird—it was already there). In the late 1600's Englishmen began to call the pie by the pet name of Mag, a short form of Margaret, and it has been "magpie" ever since.

Two species of magpies live in North America, the black-billed and yellow-billed magpies. The black-billed magpie ranges over most of the western United States and the west coast of Canada. It is also common in Europe and Asia. The yellow-billed magpie lives in California.

Magpies build huge, messy nests in the forks of trees. The nests, which are covered over like a bomb shelter, are sometimes the size of a barrel. Inside, they are very untidy, untidy enough to add a simile to English—"untidy as a magpie's nest."

"Pie" and later "magpie" were unflattering names for a noisy, blabbermouthed, or thievish person. The magpie also gave us the words "pied" (as in the Pied Piper) and "piebald." These terms originally described color combinations like the magpie's plumage. English bishops used to be called magpies by irreverent persons because of their black-and-white clothing. Some word historians also think that the kind of pie we eat was named after the magpie because its inside is as messy as a magpie's nest.

In Europe, peasants used to suspect the magpie of having evil magical powers. In Sweden it was connected with witchcraft. In parts of England, country people would spit three times over their shoulder when they saw a magpie to prevent bad luck from striking. In Scotland, superstitious folk thought that the magpie got three drops of the devil's blood every May Day, and if a magpie flew past the window of a house, someone living there would die very soon.

The Scots also had a fortune-telling rhyme about the number of magpies you might meet while out walking.

> One's sorrow, two's mirth,
> Three's a wedding, four's a birth,
> Five's a christening, six a dearth,
> Seven's heaven, eight is hell,
> And nine's the devil his ain sel'.

MEADOWLARK

Like many of the birds in this book, the meadowlark is masquerading under the name of a quite different European bird. For the meadowlark is not a lark at all, but a blackbird. It does, however, live in meadows.

The meadowlark doesn't look like a blackbird, with its bright-yellow throat and breast and dappled brown back. But it doesn't look like a lark either, for the true larks are mostly little brown or gray birds, so drab you can hardly see them until you are almost stepping on them. However, like the famed skylark of Europe, the meadowlark sings as it flies (most birds sing from a perch or from the ground). And, like the larks, it lives in open country. These two similarities were probably what prompted homesick English settlers in the American colonies to name it "meadowlark."

"Meadow" is a name with a very long history. It comes from the Anglo-Saxon *maedwa,* and it can be traced back to an ancient Indo-European root, *me* (pronounced may), meaning "to mow"—that is, to cut grass for hay. So a meadow at first was a piece of land covered with grass where people mowed the hay for their cows and other farm animals. Later it came to mean a pasture as well, and finally any grassland, particularly if it was rather damp, for grass grows lushest where it has plenty of water.

"Lark" comes from the Anglo-Saxon name *laewerce* (probably pronounced lay-work-uh), which was eventually slurred into *layrkuh* and then *lark*. In the Middle Ages, there was a second form of the name, *laverock,* which is still used in Scotland. "Lark" probably comes from a very old root, because the names for the lark in the Germanic languages are very similar. For example, in Danish it is *Laerke,* in German, *Lerche,* in Swedish *lärka,* all pronounced more or less like LAYR-kuh. The French call the lark *alouette,* from the bird's Latin name, *alauda.* So when you hear the French song "Alouette, Gentille Alouette," you'll know that the singer is calling his girl friend his "nice lark."

Though Europeans used to consider larks a great delicacy —and in some European countries larks are still shot or netted for the table—they also loved them for their cheery song. The most loved was the skylark, named for its habit of singing as it soared around in the sky. While romantic English poets and writers mentioned plenty of birds, the skylark tops the list. A famous poem named "To a Skylark," by Percy Bysshe Shelley, is still popular, though it was written more than 150 years ago.

The name "lark" was also given to some birds that were not larks. In fact, in England the name "meadowlark" refers to a kind of pipit, a small, dull-colored bird that looks rather like a lark and twitters as it flies.

True larks are found over a vast area of Europe, Asia, and Africa, but only one species, the horned lark, is found in America. The horned lark is named for two small tufts of feathers that stick up like horns on either side of its head.

Many birds of the New World could not stand the changes made by European settlers who destroyed their natural habitats of woods and swamps and prairies. The meadowlark was not one of these. The more woods that were cut down and turned into open fields, the better the meadowlarks liked it, for their natural habitat is open country. And along with fields and pastures came more of the insects and seeds that meadowlarks feed on. In North America there are two species of meadowlarks, which look so much alike that they are hard to tell apart. The eastern meadowlark ranges from the Atlantic coast to west of the Mississippi River, and the western meadowlark ranges from the Pacific coast east to the Mississippi. So there is a belt where the two overlap. However, they do not interbreed, because the females of each species ignore the courting song of the males of the other species.

When settlers moved out onto the Great Plains, they faced a new kind of world that was quite strange. For miles and miles there were no trees—just an endless seas of grass or grain fields as far as the eye could see. The familiar songbirds were missing. But they found one old friend, the meadowlark, whose song made them feel at home. A favorite bird of the settlers, the meadowlark became the state bird of six states: Kansas, Nebraska, North Dakota, Oregon, Montana, and Wyoming.

The eastern meadowlark's scientific name is *Sturnella*

magna, which means "big little starling." Actually it is an ornithological blooper, for the meadowlark is not related to the starlings. The western meadowlark's scientific name is *Sturnella neglecta*, or "neglected little starling," because for many years it was not recognized as a species in its own right—except by eastern meadowlarks—and so was "neglected" by scientists.

"We just did it for a lark" used to be a favorite explanation of young people up to more or less harmless mischief. This meaning of "lark" may have come partly from the playful antics of larks in flight, but the dictionaries trace it to a North of England dialect word, "lake," meaning "to play." "Lark" in the sense of "prank" dates back to the early 1800's. Another expression, "skylarking," meaning "fooling around," began as sailors' slang about the same time. Perhaps it was first used to describe the antics of young seamen clowning around in the rigging, far above the deck.

MOCKINGBIRD

The dull, gray mockingbird would take no beauty prizes, but it has one of the best singing voices in the bird world, plus an unexcelled talent for mimicking the songs of other birds. It is this talent for mimicry that gave it its name.

"Mock" came into the English language in the 1400's as a word borrowed from French. Originally it meant "to hold up to ridicule" or "to make fun of." Later it took on the added meaning of ridiculing someone by imitating him, and from there it also came to mean imitating or counterfeiting. When English settlers in the Southern colonies in the early 1600's discovered a bird that could mimic the calls of many other birds, they quite naturally called it the mock-bird. The present form, "mockingbird," dates back to 1676.

Modern ornithologists have found that some mockingbirds have a repertory of the songs and calls of more than thirty other birds. When they took sonagrams of the mockingbirds' imitations and compared them to the sounds of the real birds, the sonagrams were almost impossible to tell apart, so exactly did the mockingbirds duplicate the sounds of the other birds.

Mockingbirds imitate not only other songbirds, but also chickens, turkeys, cats, dogs, squeaky wheels, and phonograph records. One mockingbird supposedly liked to listen to people playing the piano and later sing back as much of the piano melody as it could manage. The scientific name of the mockingbird, *Mimus polyglottos*, pays respect to the bird's talent for mimicry. It means "many-tongued mimic."

In its own right, the mocking bird sings as beautifully as the nightingale (in fact, mockingbirds have been known to imitate caged nightingales perfectly). Mockingbirds are no shy songsters. They perch on open branches, telephone

wires, fence posts, roofs, TV aerials, and chimney tops to sing. They sing at any time of the day and also on moonlit nights, when the effect is especially romantic—at least on human listeners.

Mockingbirds range from the Atlantic to the Pacific coast and as far north as southern New York State and the southern fringe of New England. But they are most numerous in the Southeastern states, and they are one of the traditional symbols of the South. Five Southern states claim the mockingbird as their state bird: Arkansas, Florida, Mississippi, Tennessee, and Texas.

Mockingbirds are by nature woodland birds, but they often build their nests close to houses, for they are not afraid of man. They defend their nests fearlessly against cats, dogs, and other birds and will even attack people who come too close to the nest, but otherwise are friendly toward man. Some mockingbirds become so tame that they will come into the house through an open door or window to be fed.

Closely related to the mockingbird are the catbird and the brown thrasher, which is the state bird of Georgia.

The brown thrasher gets its name partly because it is cinnamon-brown in color and partly because of its habit of thrashing its long tail up and down when it is nervous or angry. Another explanation is that "thrasher" is a corruption of "thrusher," an old dialect version of "thrush." Although the thrasher is not a thrush, it is often mistaken for one because of its spotted breast. The thrasher sings almost as well as the mockingbird, and it is also a good mimic, although its repertory is more limited than its cousin's. A thrasher's mimic song can easily be told from a mockingbird's because the thrasher repeats the song only once, while the mockingbird runs through it several times.

ORIOLE

Every spring, birds with rich yellow-and-black plumage fly north to Europe's woods and fields, like a ray of sunshine after the long, gray winter. Hundreds of years ago, someone gave these brightly colored birds the name of *aureolus*, which is Latin for "little golden one." Today we know them as golden orioles.

In France, the name *aureolus* was gradually shortened to *oriol*, and English naturalists eventually took this name over, adding an *e* to the end. However, though golden orioles were common over large parts of Europe, they very seldom crossed the sea to England, so the bird had no name at all in English until the late 1700's.

In the 1700's the study of nature for its own sake was really just getting under way, and European naturalists were having a field day studying and classifying plants and animals (including birds) from all over the world. So when they discovered birds in North America that looked very much like the familiar golden orioles of Europe, they named them orioles too. Actually, the birds are not related, for American orioles are related to blackbirds and grackles, while European orioles are most closely related to crows and jays.

American orioles spend their winters in the tropics and come north in late spring to build their nests. More than six species of orioles spend their summers in the United States. Some are yellow and black, but the most familiar kinds are orange and black: the Baltimore oriole, the orchard oriole, and Bullock's oriole, which lives in the West.

The Baltimore oriole was named for its orange-and-black coloring, for these were the colors of the Baltimores, the family of powerful English noblemen who founded the colony of Maryland in 1632 and 1633. (The city of Baltimore is also named after the Baltimores.) The Baltimores began as a plain English family named Calvert. One of them went into politics and served the king well—so well that the grateful monarch rewarded him by making him the lord of Baltimore, a town in the south of Ireland. The newly created lord also asked the king to grant him the right to found a colony in North America. Before the charter was approved, the first Lord Baltimore died, but his son took over and sent the first shipload of settlers in 1633. Since the Baltimores were so important in Maryland history (they ruled the colony, off and on, until 1771), the bird that wore their colors was named the state bird of Maryland. The Baltimore baseball team also bears the proud name of Orioles. However, the Baltimore oriole is not limited to Maryland. It ranges north into Canada and west far beyond the Mississippi River.

Only the male orioles are brightly colored. The females are rather dull; their color helps conceal them from predators. The females are the ones that build the unusual cup-shaped or pouch-shaped hanging nests for which orioles are famous. Once they have found a suitable tree, they gather long grass stems, pieces of string, and other fibers and weave them skillfully into a nest hanging from a forked twig. The Baltimore oriole's nest, a six-inch-deep pouch, looks rather like an old sock that has somehow found its way high up into a tree. These hanging nests gave orioles an old-time name of "hangbirds."

When scientists realized that American orioles were not related to European orioles, they had to invent a new name for them. The name that they chose for the oriole genus was

Icterus. It was a peculiar choice, for the name comes from the Greek word for jaundice, a disease in which the victim's skin turns a dull, sickly yellow. It does no justice to the bright, gay colors of the orioles. Later on, the name of Icteridae was given to the whole family of orioles, grackles, cowbirds, and blackbirds. So the shiny, black blackbird belongs to the family of "jaundice-yellow birds."

Orioles are appreciated for their clear, cheery song as well as for their gay colors. In many of the Northern states, the oriole's song is one of the first signs that summer has really come. Orioles also eat large quantities of destructive insects, which should make them even more appreciated.

OWL

Owl comes from the Anglo-Saxon *ule*, which was probably an imitation of the bird's hooting. Some of the owl's names in other languages also sound like attempts to mimic its hoots, for example, *ulula* (Latin), *Eule* and *Uhu* (German), and *uggla* (Swedish). All these names probably go back to an old root meaning "to howl." Indeed, another name for the owl in Old England was *howl* or *howlet*.

Actually, not all owls hoot. Some wail; some cluck; some cackle. The screech owl has a soft, quavering whistle. All owls express annoyance or anger by clacking their bills. Owl couples often call back and forth to each other in "duets" that can last for hours. In some species the males and females have different calls.

Owls were once thought to be related to hawks because of their sharp, hooked bills, powerful talons, and predatory way of life. However, they are not related. Owls' closest relatives are the whippoorwills and goatsuckers. The owls' resemblance to hawks came about because both groups of birds specialized in preying on creatures big enough to put up some fight. So owls and hawks both developed talons to hold and kill their prey and powerful, hooked beaks for tearing flesh. But while hawks hunt during the daytime, owls long ago turned to working the night shift. In this way they avoided competing directly with the hawks.

Owls are beautifully adapted for nighttime hunting. Their wings make no noise as they fly. Some scientists say that this is to avoid alarming their prey by the noise of wing beats; others say it is to keep from interfering with the owl's sensitive hearing, which enables it to locate animals in pitch-dark, as inside a barn. Owls' eyes are extremely sensitive to light, so that they see well at night. They are the only birds whose eyes are set side by side, facing forward like a human's. This gives them stereoscopic vision and depth perception. However, owls have very little side vision, because their eyeballs are virtually immovable in their sockets. An owl cannot look out of the corner of its eye. To look to the right or left, it must turn its whole head.

An owl's neck is so flexible that it can turn its head a full half circle or a little more. If you walk around an owl perched on a branch, it will follow you with its head as far as it can turn, then snap its head around the other way to keep following you. It does this with such lightning speed that it can hardly be seen, so people used to believe that an owl could turn its head in a complete circle. Country people claimed that you could catch an owl by walking around it in circles until its head came loose from turning to watch you and fell off.

Another old belief was that owls are blind in daylight. This is not true. Owls see perfectly well by daylight, although they generally hunt at night. But there are owls that do most of their hunting in the daytime. These are species that live in the far north, where daylight lasts almost all around the clock in summer and where there are no hawks to compete with them.

Owls eat mice, rabbits, gophers, other birds, snakes, frogs, and insects. Some owls also catch fish. The bigger the owl, the bigger the kinds of animals it preys on. Owls sometimes make pests of themselves by raiding man's chickens and turkeys, but they do immense good by keeping down the numbers of mice and other rodents.

The biggest owl in North America is the great gray owl, which is rare in the United States. It measures nearly two feet long and has a five-foot wingspread. Almost as large is the great horned owl, named for the hornlike tufts of feathers on each side of its head. Another big owl is the snowy owl, which lives in the Arctic and is almost pure white, with dark speckles, to blend with a snow-covered landscape. It sometimes comes down to the northern United States in winter.

The commonest owls are the foot-long barn owl and the eight-inch screech owl, which nests in hollow trees. The smallest owl is the elf owl, which lives in the deserts of the southwestern United States. It nests in holes in giant cactus plants and lives mostly on insects. On the Great Plains lives the burrowing owl, which often moves into prairie-dog tunnels. The owls occasionally eat prairie dogs, and the prairie dogs sometimes eat the owls' eggs, but most of the time they do not molest each other.

Until modern times, people feared owls as birds of the night and believed they were in league with demons and witches. It was thought that an owl's cry heralded someone's death. If an owl came out by day and hooted, that was a sure sign of disaster, such as defeat in a battle, destruction of a city by earthquake or fire, or an invasion of armed barbarians.

But feared as they were, owls were also used as magical charms against all sorts of calamities. The idea was probably that the demonic bird could frighten off other demons that caused sickness and accident. (To primitive peoples, nothing bad ever happened naturally. It was always caused by an evil spirit or by witchcraft.) In China, figures of owls were put on rooftops to keep lightning away. In Germany, real owls were nailed to doors for the same purpose. In the North of England, owl broth was supposed to cure whooping cough. In the 1600's, learned English physicians believed that feeding a drunkard owl's eggs would cure him of his

addiction to liquor. The Romans believed that the ashes of burned owls' feet would cure snakebite.

The ancient Greeks made the owl sacred to Athene, the goddess of wisdom. This gave the owl a great but undeserved reputation as the wisest of birds, for it is actually a rather stupid bird and easy to fool. But the owl appears wise to humans because it sits still and grave and says nothing. Many people have earned a reputation for wisdom by following the owl's example. Perhaps they deserved it for being clever enough to keep their mouths shut!

PELICAN

Almost everyone knows the silly rhyme "A wonderful bird is the Pelican/ His beak can hold more than his bellican." This much is true, and one kind of pelican can hold three gallons of stuff in the skin pouch beneath its bill, about three times the amount its stomach can hold. This pouch and a long bill are the pelican's trademarks.

The pelican uses its curious throat pouch to scoop up fish. But contrary to common belief, it does not fly home to the nest with a pouchful of fish. That would probably make it so nose-heavy it would fly straight to the bottom of the sea. Instead, the pelican swallows the fish and feeds its chicks on its partly digested stomach contents.

The pelican owes its name to the ancient Greeks, who called it *pelekan.* The Greeks called the woodpecker by a very similar name, *pelekas.* Both names seem to come from the Greek word for an ax, *pelekys.* In the case of the woodpecker, the symbolism is obvious, for the bird chops away at trees with its beak. In the case of the pelican, the Greeks may have thought that the bird cleaves the water with its beak the way an ax cleaves wood. Anyone who has seen a pelican hit the water will understand what the Greeks may have had in mind.

The Romans took over the Greek name and Latinized it to *pelecanus*. In time, the ending dropped off as Europe's languages became simpler. Modern European languages all use some form of "pelican," except for Spanish and Portuguese, which call the bird *alcatraz*. This name may have come from *al-catruz*, Arabic for "the bucket," which could refer to the pelican's pouch. Alcatraz Island in San Francisco Bay was named by early Spanish explorers for the pelicans that nested there. Portuguese sailors used the name *alcatraz* for all large seabirds, and so, corrupted into "albatross" by the English, it came to stand for an entirely different bird.

In the Middle Ages, Europeans thought that the pelican wounded its own breast with its bill and fed its young on the blood. Thus, the bird became a symbol of self-sacrifice and unselfish concern for others. It was worked into religious symbolism, poetry, and plays. Needless to say, the idea was completely mistaken. But the myth, fantastic as it was, may have been based on a tiny grain of fact. For when pelicans return to the nest from a fishing expedition, they regurgitate some of their stomach contents into their pouches. The hungry young ones stick their heads in as far as they will reach and gobble up their predigested meal. As they grow bigger, the young pelicans reach right down inside their parents' gullets. Superstitious fishermen, watching from a distance, might have thought the young ones were sucking their parents' blood. The parent birds preening their breast feathers with their beaks (necessary to keep them clean and in good shape) would have suggested the rest of the story.

Another curious belief about pelicans was that there were some kinds that lived in deserts and fed upon serpents. Again, there may be a grain of fact behind this myth, because pelicans do live in some desert areas—on salt lakes.

There are huge pelican colonies on some of the salt lakes of East Africa, which are rich in fish.

There are six species of pelicans living today, spread around the warmer regions of the world. Two are found in the New World. The white pelican lives along the west coast of the United States and on some big inland lakes. The brown pelican, which is the state bird of Louisiana, lives along the east coast from the Carolinas down to Florida, the Gulf of Mexico, and down through the West Indies to the north coast of South America. The brown pelican is actually mostly black, except for its throat and the back of its neck.

White pelicans often use teamwork in fishing. A group of the birds lines up in crescent formation on the water and swims toward shore, scaring small fish ahead of them. When the pelicans reach water too shallow for the fish to escape, they lower their beaks and scoop up their fill. Brown pelicans are solo fishermen. They soar ten to thirty feet above the water until they spot a fish, then fold their wings and plummet straight down, nose first, entering the water with a gigantic splash. They are so buoyant that they pop up again almost immediately, tail first.

Pelicans are good-sized birds. Brown pelicans average three and one half feet long and seven and one half feet from wing tip to wing tip. White pelicans run a bit over four feet long and have a wingspread of nearly ten feet. Despite their size, they are relatively light, and they have a system of air sacs under their skins that makes them unsinkable. But in spite of their light weight, pelicans have a hard time taking off. Unless the wind is right, they must run across the water, flapping their wings desperately, to get up to take-off speed.

The pelican family tree can be traced back a long way. Fossils show that pelicans have not changed basically in the last 30,000,000 or 40,000,000 years. Their closest relatives are the cormorants and the anhinga, a curious long-necked bird that dwells in Southern swamps and is often called the snakebird or water turkey.

In the air, pelicans look a bit like pterodactyls, those giant flying lizards from the days of the dinosaurs, as they flap laboriously through the air, gliding between wing beats. The young look even more reptilian, for they are hatched naked, without feathers. Their long heads and beaks give them a striking resemblance to museum artists' ideas of what pterodactyls looked like.

"Pelican" was also the name of an old piece of chemical equipment used for distilling liquids. It had a round, fat body, a "head," and a long "beak" where the distilled stuff came out.

In the 1920's "pelican" was British criminal slang for a judge, a play on the old thieves' term of "beak." Whether this amused the judges and caused them to give lighter sentences I do not know.

PHEASANT

Perhaps 3,000 years ago unknown Greek traders rowed their open boats up through the narrow straits that divide Turkey from Europe and out across the choppy waters of the Black Sea. Their destination was the kingdom of Colchis, at the eastern end of the Black Sea, rich with gold trapped from mountain streams. The men may have been pirates rather than traders, for in ancient times men often switched back and forth between the two, depending on how much of a fight they thought the other side could put up. After a long journey they reached Colchis and rowed up the wide river which they called Phasis until they reached the capital of the kingdom. There they did their business of trading or raiding and returned home. Among the treasures they brought back with them were colorful birds with long, plumelike tail feathers—pheasants. The Greeks back home, who had never seen such birds, called them *Phasianos ornis*, the "Phasian bird," from the region of the Phasis River where they ran wild. The Greeks raised the birds in captivity and, as they grew familiar with them, dropped the *ornis* ("bird") from the name, feeling that anyone would know a Phasian was a bird, just as farmers today know that a Jersey or a Holstein-Friesian is a cow, or a Poland-China a pig, or a Rhode Island Red a chicken.

The unknown Greek traders may have been the legendary Argonauts. There really was a kingdom of Colchis, and many scholars believe that the story of the Argonauts' raid there was based on events that really happened, even though it grew mightily during the telling and retelling.

The Romans learned from the Greeks how to raise pheasants, and they also took over the Greek name, changing it slightly to *phasianus* to make it sound respectably Latin and not suspiciously foreign. The Romans were fond of pheasants, for they make excellent eating, and they spread them across their empire in Europe. Thanks to Roman pheasant breeders, the names for the pheasant in modern European languages are very similar: French, *faisan*; German, *Fasan*; Spanish, *faisan*; Swedish, *fasan*; Italian, *fagiano*. The English name "pheasant" comes from the Old French name *fesant*, which was brought in by the Normans. But there were probably pheasants in England long before the Normans conquered it in 1066, brought in by the Romans more than 500 years earlier.

Some of the Romans' pheasants escaped and went wild, surviving best where there were grasslands and grainfields to feed them and hedges or brush to hide in, for pheasants are not birds of the deep forests. Many aristocrats kept on raising them in order to let them loose for hunting, for in this way they could be sure of a dependable supply. King Henry VIII of England kept a French priest on his payroll as a "fesaunt breder."

The first pheasants were brought to the United States in the 1790's by a wealthy New Jersey man who hoped to set up a grand estate in the English fashion. Unfortunately, the birds did not survive their first winter. Later attempts to import pheasants also failed. Although the birds thrived in captivity, they disappeared once they were turned out on their own. Perhaps American predators were too much for them; perhaps the climate was wrong. Not until the 1880's, when ring-necked pheasants were brought to Oregon from northern China, did the experiment succeed. The ringnecks multiplied so successfully that they can now be found wild over much of the northern United States and southern Canada. Wild pheasants live less than thirty miles from the edge of New York City. Ring-necked pheasants are also raised on "farms" in many states. They have thrived best in the northern Plains states, which are most like their ancestral home in Asia. The two Dakotas probably have the greatest number of pheasants, and the ring-necked pheasant is the state bird of South Dakota.

The pheasant is one of the Galliformes, or "chicken-shaped birds," and so is related to the turkey, guinea hen, grouse, quail, and many other birds. The chicken itself is a pheasant, descended from the wild jungle fowl of southern Asia.

The common pheasant—the kind that the Greeks brought back from Colchis—originally ranged from southwestern Asia to China and Korea. The ringneck is a variety of this species. Most of the fifty-odd species of pheasants are native to Asia. Some of them are very beautiful. The golden pheasant of central China, for instance, has a golden head and back, bright-red breast and belly, wings of red, blue, and brown, tiger-striped neck feathers, and mottled coppery-brown and black tail feathers. The impeyan pheasant, which lives in the Himalaya Mountains, is a symphony of irides-cent green, blue, and black, with patches of red and gold, and coppery tail feathers. The Lady Amherst pheasant, from Tibet and Burma, is mostly silver, green, and blue, with dashes of red and gold and black-and-silver striped tail feathers that are twice as long as its body. These beautiful pheasants and others can often be seen at zoos.

The splendid tail plumes of the pheasants sometimes give them an unusual length—the Lady Amherst pheasant averages fifty inches from beak to tail tip; the giant Argus pheasant reaches six feet, and the black-and-gold Reeves pheasant can reach eight feet. Scientists believe that these long tail plumes were developed to help the males compete for females, but that this sexual selection went too far, for the outsized feathers get in the birds' way and hinder them from evading predators. This, many scientists think, is the reason why the beautiful Asian pheasants are so rare.

PIGEON

Pigeon comes from *pipio*, the Latin word for a peeping, cheeping baby bird. (*Pipire* meant "to peep," and a *pipio* was a little bird that *pipire*'d.) In French, *pipio* was transformed into *pyjoun*, and it gradually came to mean a baby pigeon rather than baby birds in general. The French, like many other people, were fond of pigeons as part of their dinner. Since baby pigeons were better eating than old ones, cooks probably called all the pigeons they served up "pyjouns" regardless of their age, to persuade their masters that they were young and tender. And so "pyjoun" came to cover all pigeons, not just young ones. After the Normans conquered England, the French *pyjoun* fluttered into the English language alongside the older name of *dove*. By the time

Christopher Columbus made his first voyage, Englishmen were using "pigeon" as an everyday word.

Columbus' real name, by the way, was Colombo, the Italian word for "pigeon" (from *columba*, the Latin name). If history writers had translated his name into English, we would now be reading about the discoveries of Christopher Pigeon and watching parades on Pigeon Day.

The modern name for a baby pigeon is "squab," which dates from the 1600's. "Squab" probably came from an old word meaning "fat man," for squabs are about as fat as they can be without bursting.

"Dove" probably comes from the Scandinavian word *duva* and was brought into English by Danish invaders who settled in England about 200 years before the Normans took over. "Dove" and "pigeon" have been used interchangeably for centuries. There is a kind of loose rule that the smaller kinds of pigeons are called doves and the bigger ones pi-

geons, but which one you use is really a matter of custom and choice.

The pigeons are a very large family of birds, with nearly three hundred species. Pigeons are found in all parts of the world except the coldest regions. The largest pigeons live in the islands of the South Pacific. Some of them measure almost three feet long, counting the tail feathers. (By way of comparison, our common city pigeons measure thirteen inches, and millions of city dwellers think that is thirteen inches too much.)

Pigeons are unusual in several ways. They are the only birds that can drink by sucking up water into their beaks. Other birds must take a beakful and tilt their heads back to swallow. Pigeons feed their young on a milky fluid, called pigeon's milk, which they secrete in their crops. No other birds have the ability to secrete "milk." And pigeons have an extraordinary homing sense that enables them to find their way home over many miles of strange country. Man took advantage of this homing instinct and for several thousand years used trained pigeons to carry messages. Until two-way radio was perfected, carrier pigeons were the fastest and surest way to send messages on the battlefield.

Man probably domesticated pigeons first for food, but it almost certainly happened by chance rather than plan. When man invented agriculture and built his first settled villages and cities in the Near East, wild pigeons were nesting on nearby cliffs. Man's buildings gave the pigeons hundreds of new, artificial "cliffs" and ledges to nest on, and man's planted fields provided good feeding grounds nearby. So the pigeons moved in with no coaxing at all. It was a simple matter for prehistoric farmers to steal eggs and squabs from the nests. It didn't seem to discourage the pigeons at all. Man did not even have to give the pigeons any care. They flew off every day and found their own food and came back to their nests every night.

As civilization developed, men built great temples to honor their gods. The pigeons found the temples even more to their liking than farm buildings. Partly because they nested in temples and partly because they bred so rapidly and mated so publicly, they became sacred to various gods and symbols of fertility. Their sacredness did not prevent men from eating them—quite the contrary.

In time, men learned to build special towers on the roofs of buildings for pigeons to nest in. These towers kept large numbers of pigeons together and made it easier to harvest eggs and squabs. Some pigeon towers are still used today in Italy.

In the Middle Ages, Europeans kept pigeons in special coops called dovecotes. ("Cote" was an old form of "cottage.") The dovecote was usually put up on a pole to keep it out of reach of cats, foxes, and other predators. It was a big box divided into small compartments for the pigeons to nest in. These were the original pigeonholes. Nowadays a pigeonhole is a slot in a desk or storage shelf where papers are filed and usually forgotten.

The commonest pigeon in North America is the rock dove, which was originally imported from Europe by pigeon fanciers and found all too good a home here. The wild rock dove is the original pigeon tamed by man. It is the ancestor of all the domestic pigeons and all the domestic-pigeons-gone-wild that infest our cities.

In nature, pigeons eat seeds and fruit and sometimes leaves. In the cities, pigeons became scavengers. They found such easy pickings that they became first-rank nuisances.

Not only do their droppings befoul buildings and streets and pedestrians, but the birds carry a fungus disease that can be fatal to humans. And the loud, quarrelsome cooing of thousands of pigeons adds to the symphony of irritating noises that plague city dwellers and put their tempers on edge. In most parts of the world, city governments carry on a constant war against pigeons, without much success.

The commonest native pigeon is the mourning dove, a harmless bird that lives in farm country and suburbs. In the South, mourning doves are hunted as game birds, but in the Northern states they are protected as songbirds. The hunting is regulated so that the mourning dove is in no danger of disappearing.

One pigeon that did disappear was the passenger pigeon, whose fate was one of the great wildlife tragedies of America. The passenger pigeon once numbered in the billions. They nested in unimaginably huge flocks in the woods of the Eastern and Midwestern states and in nearby Canada. A good-sized passenger-pigeon colony could take up twenty square miles or more of woods. One big nesting ground was estimated to be three or four miles wide and forty miles long! A passenger-pigeon nesting ground was not a tidy place. The sheer weight of the birds broke off big tree limbs, and their droppings killed all vegetation on the ground. However, when the pigeons moved to another nesting ground, the forest gradually recovered. When the pigeons migrated, the sky was literally darkened by the mass of birds, which took hours to pass overhead. The sound of their wings was like a gale.

The Indians hunted passenger pigeons by the thousands. They dried and smoked the adult birds and boiled down the squabs for oil. But there were not enough Indians to make a dent in the pigeon population. It took the businesslike, efficient white man to manage that. White hunters invaded the nesting grounds and engaged in orgies of slaughtering the helpless birds. They shot them, trapped them in nets and clubbed them to death, and sometimes chopped down nesting trees to get the fat young squabs that could not fly yet. The cruelty of the hunters was revolting.

Squabs were packed into barrels and sent by the freight-car load to the cities, where they were sold as a delicacy. It seemed as if the supply of pigeons would never end. If they were wiped out in one state, there were always more farther west. And some pigeons always escaped the hunters to raise more young. What the hunters did not know—and might not have cared about if they had known—was that passenger pigeons' instincts were "programmed" so that they could breed only in huge colonies. If five or six hundred birds escaped, they simply would not breed. They required the stimulus of many thousands of their own kind around them. The last great passenger-pigeon nesting colony, in Michigan, was destroyed in 1878. After that, the remaining birds faded rapidly away. The last surviving passenger pigeon in the world died in the Cincinnati Zoo in 1914. With it died a magnificent species that can never be brought back.

Pigeons are not very intelligent birds, and their stupidity made "pigeon" a nickname for an easily deceived person; such as the victim of a crooked gambler. Wild pigeons were often caught with the aid of a tame decoy pigeon, called a stool pigeon. In the 1800's, criminals in Britain and the United States gave this name to underworld characters who passed information to the police. Worse yet, "pigeon-livered" means "cowardly."

It would seem from these expressions that mankind has no

great love for the pigeon. But for thousands of years the dove has been the symbol of peace and gentleness and innocence, and a dove was one of the birds that Noah sent out from the Ark to see if the Flood had stopped in the Bible story. "Dove" has been a pet name between lovers for as long as man has been writing poetry. And the amorous cooing and cuddling of pigeons has made "lovey-dovey" proverbial.

QUAIL

Quail comes from the Old French *quaille*, which probably came from a still older Germanic name that was something like *quackel*, an imitation of the bird's call. This name can still be traced in some modern European languages: Dutch, *kwakkel*; German, *Wachtel*; Swedish, *vaktel*; French, *caille*; Italian, *quaglia*. The Greek name for the quail was *ortyx*, which crops up in many of the scientific names for various kinds of quail. The Romans called the succulent little bird *coturnix*, which has come down to modern times as the Spanish *codorniz*.

Quails belong to the family called Galliformes, or "chicken-shaped birds." Their closest relatives are partridges, pheasants, and chickens, and some of the quails look very much like plump little chickens without a comb. Quails are very good eating, and since prehistoric times man has relished them.

Quails have a very ancient history. Primitive hunters, watching the birds' frenzied mating antics in spring, made the quail into a symbol of sex and fertility. In ancient Greece and in the Middle East the quail was also a symbol of the return of spring, for in springtime the quails flew up out of Africa in flocks of millions, fanning out to their breeding grounds in Europe and Asia. The Bible tells how the Jewish tribes, wandering in the desert of Sinai after escaping from Egypt, were saved from starvation by one of these huge flights of quails.

The spring quail migrations must have meant a feast to many a hungry peasant and herdsmen around the Mediterranean right down to modern times. The Egyptians even used to export huge numbers of quail to Europe. Around 1900 they were shipping about 2,000,000 quail a year; the high point was 1920, when 3,000,000 quail were killed and sold to Europe's gourmets. But this slaughter was too much for the quail to stand, because their numbers began to go down, and by the 1930's there weren't enough of them left to make the export business pay.

The same quails (of the *Coturnix* genus) used to migrate in just as huge numbers over eastern Asia, where they were also killed and eaten by the millions. But the Japanese were more practical than the Egyptians, for they learned how to domesticate quail and keep them in cages. Now raising quail —mainly for their eggs—is a big business in Japan, and sometimes quails' eggs are more plentiful in the market than hens' eggs.

Sportsmen have tried to raise coturnix quail in the United States, where the climate is right and there are plenty of the open woods and fields and brushland that quails live in. But each attempt failed. Although the birds grew fat and healthy, in the autumn their instincts told them to migrate south. Unfortunately, to the south lay the Gulf of Mexico, and it is believed that the birds became exhausted by the long flight and drowned.

But there are plenty of quails in the United States, six species, in fact. The most common is the bobwhite, named for its call of "Bob-bob-white!" The bobwhite ranges over most of the eastern United States and also west of the Mississippi on the Great Plains. Bobwhites also live in the far Northwest and in a little sliver of western Canada. In the South, people often call the bobwhite "partridge," and the birds do look quite alike. In fact, quails and partridges are often confused in many parts of the world.

Five species of quails live in the West. The best known is the California quail. Four of the five Western quails have a crest on their heads. The California quail has a feathery topknot shaped like an uncurled question mark. Its scientific name, *Lophortyx*, means "crested quail." It is the state bird of California, though not for this reason. The California quail has adapted well to modern conditions, and it is becoming common in some large city parks.

Quails are sociable birds. Bobwhites often form groups of as many as 100. In cold weather, they nestle together for warmth in a circle, tails together and heads facing out. In this position, they can easily spot danger, and the whole flock takes off at once like an exploding bombshell. This explosive escape may have the advantage of confusing an attacker, who cannot decide which bird to aim for. It does not help much against the wide-spraying pellets of a shotgun, however.

A flock of quails is called a covey. This term dates from the Middle Ages, when hunting was the sport of kings and nobles, and common people were not allowed to participate. Each bird and animal that was hunted had its special terminology, which took years to learn properly. This special language of hunting, like that of horsemanship, was a convenient way of telling the common herd from their "betters." "Covey" comes from the Old French word *covée*, which goes back to the Latin word *cubare*, meaning "to hatch" or "to sit on eggs."

RAVEN

Raven comes from the Anglo-Saxon *hraefn*, which was probably a clumsy imitation of the bird's deep, guttural croaking. To ancient peoples, the raven was a bird of gloom and doom and death. Its coal-black feathers made it a bird of the night, when imaginary demons and real wild beasts roamed the world, and its deep, sepulchral tones sounded like a voice from a tomb. Possibly it was a demon itself, or so many ancient peoples believed. At the very least, they were convinced that evil spirits sometimes took the form of ravens.

Actually the raven is quite an ordinary bird except for its size. It is the giant of the crow family, reaching twenty-six inches from beak to tail tip, about one-third again as large as the common crow. Ravens were once found all over the Northern Hemisphere, in homes as different as the Sahara Desert, the Scottish highlands, and the sea cliffs of the northwestern United States. Nowadays ravens have retreated to the places where men are least common. In America, these are mainly the high mountains of the West, Alaska, and Canada north of the tree line.

In the ancient Near East, ravens were considered unclean birds because of their habit of eating carrion. They are among the birds listed as forbidden food in the Bible. But they could be creatures of good, too. A raven was one of the birds that Noah sent out from the Ark to see if the Great Flood of the Bible was ended. And ravens fed the prophet Elijah when he hid in the wilderness from the anger of the wicked King Ahab.

The Greeks believed that the raven was sacred to Apollo, the god of the sun. But this did not mean too much, because Apollo had a whole regiment of sacred animals, even field mice. The raven was much more important to the ancient Norsemen, for it belonged to their chief god, Odin, who was sometimes called the Raven God. Odin had a pair of ravens that sat on his shoulders wherever he went and served as his messengers and spies. They were called Hugin and Munin, Thought and Memory. Odin himself sometimes took the shape of a raven.

In the Middle Ages and even down to modern times there were many superstitions about ravens. A raven's croak was supposed to foretell death, the outcome of a battle, and other fateful things. In parts of France, it was whispered that wicked priests turned to ravens when they died. At the

Tower of London there is a small flock of ravens supported by the government. Tradition says that when there are no more ravens at the Tower, the downfall of Britain will come. Some people still take this seriously enough to be worried if one of the ravens dies.

Danish Vikings had a raven on their battle flags, and the raven was supposed to spread its wings and raise its head if the Danes were going to be victorious. If the battle was to be lost, it would droop its wings and head. The flagmakers must have taken extra care to paint the ravens looking extremely confident and victorious.

Ravens can be tamed and taught to speak a few words. It was for this reason that Edgar Allan Poe chose one to play the lead role in his famous poem "The Raven." As Poe explained it, he wanted to write a poem of about 100 lines with

the themes of grief and melancholy. This would please both the public *and* the critics (never easy to do). He decided that the poem needed a keynote to tie it together, a refrain to come at the end of each verse. After trying out many combinations of sounds, he settled on "nevermore" as the best word for creating the mood he wanted. Then he needed some reason for repeating this word so many times. He decided that it must be spoken by some nonreasoning creature capable of speech, such as a parrot. But a parrot is a rather comical creature, not at all suitable for the gloomy, high-toned poem he had in mind. What other bird could talk? Of course, a tame raven! Having disposed of the most important questions, Poe proceeded to work out the rest of the poem, and it became an instant success.

ROADRUNNER

The roadrunner lives in the arid Southwest and Mexico. Although it looks a bit like a blown-up, rumpled woodpecker, it is actually a giant, ground-dwelling cuckoo. So well adapted is the roadrunner to life on the ground that it has almost lost the power of flight, and it is about all the bird can manage to flap its way up to its nest in a mesquite bush or a tall cactus. However, on the ground it can trot along easily at fifteen miles per hour, faster than most of the predators that might attack it and much faster than the snakes and lizards it eats itself. The roadrunner also varies its diet with snacks of insects, spiders, and mice, which it dispatches with a blow of its powerful, spearlike bill.

135

The scientific name of the roadrunner is *Geococcyx californianus*, meaning "Californian ground-cuckoo." The "Californian" part of the name came about because the specimen which the scientists named came from that state. Despite California's claim, the roadrunner is the state bird of New Mexico.

"Road" comes from the Anglo-Saxon word *rad*, which comes from *ridan*, meaning "to ride." Once "road" meant the act of riding, and only much later did it come to mean the path or track that one rides along. "Run" comes from the Anglo-Saxon *rinnan*, meaning "to run." The roadrunner got its name from its habit of running along the roads built by early settlers in the Southwest. Crude as they were, they still made travel easier than dodging through the brush. Today roadrunners get an additional benefit from roads: the snakes, lizards, and other small animals killed by traffic.

Almost every American has seen the cartoon "Roadrunner," whizzing along the highway with incredible speed and shouting "Meep-meep!" as he outwits the fiendish schemes of his enemy the Coyote. In real life, however, the roadrunner does not honk like an automobile, but sings a soft, dove-like song as it struts about the mesquite looking for a meal.

ROBIN

The robin's name is a double mistake. For one thing, the American robin is not at all the same bird as the original European robin. For another, "robin" was not a real name to begin with. It was an Old French nickname for Robert, like our modern "Bobby." After the Norman conquest of England, Robin became a common English nickname.

Some time before 1450 Englishmen began to use the name for a small bird they called the redbreast on account of the reddish chest feathers of the male birds. "Robin redbreast" became a popular name; in fact, it is still used today. Later, people began to drop the "redbreast" part of the name and use only the "robin." It was as if we called sparrows "Sammy sparrow" and then simply "sammy."

When English colonists came to North America, they found a bird that looked rather like the familiar English robin, red breast and all, although it was twice as large. So they called it robin too. Actually the two birds are not closely related, although both belong to the thrush family. They are different in many ways.

European robins were greatly loved by the people. In most countries of Europe people made up stories and poems about them. This did not keep the people from trapping the birds and eating them, for roasted robins were a highly esteemed delicacy.

European robins spend their summers in the north and fly south for the winter. Some travel as far south as oases in the Sahara Desert. American robins also migrate south for the winter, returning to the Northern states in early spring to claim their territories and build nests. The first robin was a sign of spring, just as surely as the first appearance of the ice-cream man. But after World War II millions of Americans moved to suburbs, where they had houses with back yards. In these back yards many of them set up bird feeders to keep birds from starving during the hard winter months. The free lunches available at the bird feeders lured some robins to stay on all through the winter, so the sight of a robin does not always mean that spring is on its way. He may never have left in the fall.

In many European countries the robin is known by names that mean "redbreast." And the red breast of the male is certainly conspicuous. But it is not there just to look beautiful. Its real purpose is to signal other male robins "Get off my territory!" Robins are so strongly programmed to react to red that scientists have seen them threaten a bunch of red feathers or a piece of red cloth. One robin even threatened some tomatoes it noticed ripening in a window.

The robin's cheery springtime song has the same purpose as the red breast. When two male robins are competing for the same territory, each will puff himself up as large as he can and sing with all his force. This allows the birds to "fight" symbolically without either one getting injured. Eventually, one robin gives way and slinks off, and the other triumphantly claims the territory. The bird that wins the territory also wins the female, which is the real reason for the contest.

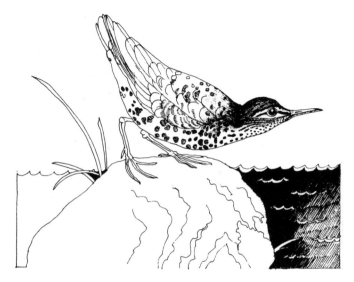

SANDPIPER

The sandpiper is a little shorebird that calls in a high, piping voice as it scurries along the sand of the beach looking for food. So its name makes rare good sense. "Sand" has come down unchanged from Anglo-Saxon times. "Piper" comes from the Latin verb *pipare*, meaning "to peep" or "to chirp." And a *pipa* (pronounced peep-ah) was a musical instrument that made peeping, chirping sounds. These words passed into the Germanic languages along with many others. In Old English, a *pipere* was someone who played the pipes or made a peeping noise, like the sandpiper.

Some of the sandpipers make almost unbelievably long trips from their summer breeding grounds to their wintering grounds. The pectoral sandpiper, which breeds in the Arctic, migrates as far as the southern tip of Argentina, a distance of about 10,000 miles, for it does not travel in a straight line. Migrating sandpipers often stop off at airports and golf courses—not to make flight reservations or to play golf, but to hunt for insects in the close-cut grass.

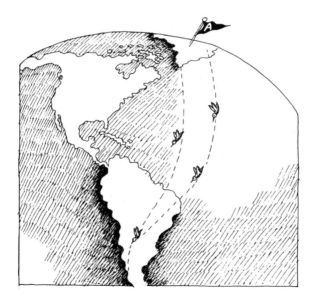

SNIPE

The snipe is a close relative of the sandpipers and plovers. It could be called an inland sandpiper that lives in marshes and bogs and along riverbanks. The snipe is known for its long bill, with which it probes the ground for food. All the snipes (there are a dozen species, of which one is common in North America) have a spectacular mating flight. The male circles high in the air and zooms down over the female, tail feathers spread out like a fan.

The snipe's name may come from an old Scandinavian word, *snipa*, which carried the meaning of "snip" or "snap," which is what the long beak does when the bird finds something to eat. The Germans call the snipe a *Schnepfe*. The Italian name is *beccaccino*, which may mean "little beaky," for *becco* is the word for "beak." The scientific name for the snipes is *Capella*, which is Latin for "little female goat." Eighteenth-century scholars must have strained their imagination to come up with this name, for the snipe bears not the slightest resemblance to the bleating, horned quadruped.

But there may be a faint link with ancient mythology and folklore. In its mating flight, the male snipe makes a loud noise, caused by air rushing through its wing and tail feathers, that can sound like the booming drumroll of distant thunder. To the primitive tribes that lived in part of northern Europe, any bird that could make a noise like thunder must have a magic power to cause real thunder. In fact, it must have some kind of link to the thunder god. So they named the bird "Thunder's she-goat," for the goat was one of the thunder god's favorite animals. Since scientists in the eighteenth century liked to pick names from mythology, they may have picked up this ancient bit of lore.

Since snipes live in wet, muddy places, people sometimes called them guttersnipes, for one of the old meanings of "gutter" was "muck" or "filth." About 100 years ago "guttersnipe" became an insulting name for broken-down bums who picked trash and garbage from street gutters. Then it became a term for the gangs of neglected slum children who roamed the streets making a living by petty thievery. It is still used as a term of reproach to people who behave badly.

"Snipe" also became a slang word for used cigar and cigarette butts, perhaps because they were smoked by guttersnipes who picked them up off the street.

"Sniping" in the military sense of a hidden sharpshooter picking off enemy soldiers probably comes from the sport of snipe shooting. Snipes are tasty birds, and snipe hunting was popular in the United States, as well as in Europe. Old hunt-

143

ing books went into great detail on the best way to approach snipe without alarming them, the kind of clothes to wear into their muddy haunts, the best size of shot to knock the birds down without blowing them to inedible shreds, and so on.

But the "snipe hunt" was also a practical joke known to nearly every American boy who ever went to summer camp. The hunt was held at night. The jokers would tell the victim —a new, inexperienced camper—that they needed him to help them capture the elusive bird. Full of joy at being accepted by his campmates, the new kid agreed to go. The "hunters" explained that they would all go out in the woods where the snipe lived. Then the victim was to stay in one place, equipped with a flashlight and a burlap sack, while the others fanned out and banged on trees and bushes with sticks to drive the snipe toward him. When the snipe appeared, the victim was to plop the sack over it and hold it till the others came to him. Of course, the others never came. They trotted off, made a little noise, and then sneaked back to camp, while the poor victim stayed out half the night until he finally caught on to the trick.

SPARROW

In 1850 someone imported eight pairs of house sparrows from England and turned them loose in a Brooklyn cemetery. It was the worst mistake ever made by a birdlover. The English sparrow turned into the worst bird pest the United States has known.

In 1850 no one expected this, of course. In its European home the house sparrow was not particularly objectionable. It was a perky, assertive little bird that could hold its own wherever man thrived—on farms, in country villages, and even in smoke-choked industrial cities. Although it could sometimes be a nuisance, natural forces kept it in balance with the rest of the world. But when it was brought to the

United States, the natural checks were missing, and the sparrows multiplied at a fantastic rate.

Hordes of sparrows numbering in the millions infested cities and towns. Their nests choked rain gutters, causing roofs to leak. Sparrow filth contaminated the water in storage tanks. The birds' droppings coated the sides of the buildings where they roosted. They pecked holes in fruits, stole

seeds from gardens, and raided farmers' grainfields. Worse yet, from a bird lover's viewpoint, they crowded out desirable native birds such as bluebirds, martins, robins, and thrushes. Aptly compared to rats with feathers, the aggressive sparrows ate most of the available food and chased the native birds away. As they stayed around Northern cities all winter, they were able to move into the good nesting sites before the native birds returned from the South. And they raised not one but several broods of young a year. The result was that the native birds practically disappeared wherever the sparrows took hold.

House sparrows' natural food is seeds and insects, but they will eat practically anything. According to a story that is hard to verify, they were first brought to the United States to stop a plague of tent caterpillars that were destroying trees in city parks and cemeteries and that native birds won't touch. The sparrows weren't very interested either, for they could find plentiful food supplies in the city streets. They grew fat on the grain that spilled from horses' nosebags (this was before the gasoline engine replaced the horse as the source of power for urban transportation). They even picked over the horse manure that littered the streets for bits of undigested grain. And kindhearted people unwisely threw stale breadcrumbs to the pathetic-looking little birds. But when horses disappeared from city streets, the sparrows' main food supply was cut off, and their numbers decreased somewhat.

Brooklyn was not the only community to import English sparrows. Other cities followed Brooklyn's example. But soon there was no need to bring sparrows from the other side of the ocean. There were more than enough right on hand.

But not all sparrows are villains. The native American sparrows (about thirty species) are useful, nondestructive birds. Some of them have pleasing songs. They live in every kind of habitat from marsh to desert. The song sparrow and the chipping sparrow (named for its call, "chip-chip-chip") often nest in backyard shrubbery. Another common species is the white-throated sparrow, sometimes called the Peabody bird. Old-timers thought it called "Old Sam Peabody, Peabody, Peabody!" Tree sparrows (which spend most of their time on the ground) are common winter visitors to the United States. They often turn up at bird feeders.

The name "sparrow" comes from the Anglo-Saxon name *spearwe*, which at one time was apparently a general name for small, fluttering birds. Later on it was narrowed down to a few related birds belonging to the finch family. One, in particular, came to be known as the house sparrow, because it hung around houses and farm buildings, or simply *the* sparrow, because it was by far the commonest sparrow in England. In the United States it is often called the English sparrow because it was originally imported from England. "House sparrow" is a better name, however, because the bird lives over most of Europe and Asia.

The sparrow was a popular character in the animal stories that peasants used to tell. Sometimes it was a villain, serving the devil as a watchman. In the old folk rhyme "Who Killed Cock Robin?" the sparrow was the murderer. But usually the sparrow was a hero. The peasants, helpless under the power of their overlords, loved to hear of the little, insignificant sparrow triumphing over such powerful and greedy enemies as wolves, bears, and eagles, which stood for noblemen, knights, and other people who mistreated them.

STARLING

Starling comes from the Anglo-Saxon name *staerlinc*, which was made up from *staer*, an older Anglo-Saxon name for the bird, plus the ending *ling*, which carried the meaning of "little." It has nothing to do with "star." But the starling starred in a success story gone out of control. Next to the English sparrow, the common starling is the worst bird pest and the most unwelcome immigrant in the United States.

The starling story began with the best of motives. In Europe the starling is a well-liked bird, appreciated for its cheery nature, its handsome, iridescent plumage, and the numbers of harmful insects it eats. And so about a dozen attempts were made in the late 1800's to import the cheery, useful birds from Europe and start starling colonies in the United States and Canada. None succeeded until 1890, when a group of eighty starlings was released in New York City's Central Park. The birds found nesting sites to their liking under the eaves of the American Museum of Natural History, which stands just across the street from the park. They thrived and produced young. The next year another forty starlings were brought over and turned loose in the park.

For a few years, nothing remarkable happened. But then starlings began turning up in outlying parts of New York City. They crossed the Hudson River into New Jersey. They spread east into Long Island and Connecticut, up the Hudson, south and west into Delaware and Pennsylvania. All the time, the starlings were multiplying at a furious rate, and the descendants of the original birds now numbered hundreds of thousands. Like a black, twittering flood the starlings pushed on across the country, reaching California by the 1940's. By this time the authorities and the public both realized that they had a disaster on their hands, but it was too late to control the starlings. Lacking natural enemies and used to coping with man, they could not be stopped. Even such drastic measures as trapping the birds, spreading poisoned grain on the streets for them to eat, and mass shootings seemed to have no effect on the hordes of starlings that ravaged farms and infested the cities.

The trouble was that starlings are very sociable birds. When they are not nesting, they form enormous flocks, containing thousands of birds, and travel around together. One or two starlings raiding a grainfield or an orchard would make very little difference. But two or three thousand could

strip the place bare in an hour, wiping out a whole year's earnings for the farmer.

Worse yet, the starlings competed for nests and food with the native birds, which were seldom a match for them. Flickers, robins, bluebirds, wrens, and swallows were some of the victims of the tough, aggressive starlings, which also had the advantage of working in mobs, while the other birds were single. Starlings would even beat up and drive off sparrow hawks. Among all the birds their own size or smaller, only the screech owl was too tough a customer for the starlings. In addition to driving the native birds from food and nest, starlings ate their young and eggs. Only a few years after starlings had first begun to spread, bluebirds and other native species had started to disappear.

In the winter, the starlings flocked into the big cities to roost on the buildings, as they still do. Their droppings soiled buildings, streets, cars, and unlucky pedestrians, and their noisy chattering kept people awake at night. Fortunately, there are signs that the starling population explosion has come to an end, and the millions of starlings in the United States and Canada have reached a natural balance.

Following on the heels of the English sparrow disaster, the starling plague was enough to convince Congress to pass laws banning the importation of foreign species of birds, except under strict licensing regulations, and then only those species that are not able to survive in the wild. One more guest like the starling might be more than we could stand.

SWALLOW

Swallow comes from an ancient Germanic root, *swalwon*. The Anglo-Saxon version was *swealwe*, which was pronounced sway-ahl-weh. This was quite a mouthful, and eventually it was worn down to *swallow*. The swallow's name is pretty much alike in the other Germanic languages. In Swedish and Norwegian it is *svala*, in German it is *Schwalbe*, and in Dutch *zwaluw*. The Greek name, *chelidon*, and the Latin name, *hirundo*, can be found in the scientific names of several of the swallows. From *hirundo* come the French *hirondelle*, the Spanish *golondrina*, and the Italian *rondine*.

Swallows are small, insect-eating birds that are found over most of the world. Their bills are small, but their mouths open amazingly wide as they fly through the air scooping up flies and mosquitoes. Swallows spend very little time on the ground, and their legs and feet are small and weak, so that they can barely manage to shuffle along for a few feet. But in the air they are superb fliers. Many of the swallows have forked tails. The most forked of all belongs to the common barn swallow of America, Europe, and Asia.

The barn swallow is one of the birds that has benefited from man. In nature, it built its mud nests on cliff ledges and tree branches. Man's barns and sheds provided it with a much better shelter. In addition, barns were full of insects that preyed on the livestock, so the swallows had a built-in food supply. Very few barn swallows nest away from man's buildings now. Cliff swallows, another species, often nest under the eaves of buildings and on the girders of bridges. Bank swallows, which nest in the ground, tunnel into the sides of highway cuts and sandpits. Tree swallows and martins use the birdhouses man puts up to attract them.

"Martin" is a name given to some of the bigger species of swallows. The French were the first to do this. Martin used to be a very common man's name in France, in honor of the popular St. Martin, and it was given as a nickname to the bird some time during the Middle Ages. The best-known martin in the United States is the purple martin, named for the iridescent purple-blue feathers of the male.

Swallows migrate south in the fall to follow their insect food supply. They follow the warm weather back in the spring, feasting on the swarms of newly hatched insects. Thus, the swallows are one of the surest signs that summer is on its way. The swallows' regular migrations inspired many legends. In many countries people believe that the swallows return to their area on the same day each year. Actually they don't, since they depend on the coming of warm weather, which varies from year to year. But legends die hard, and plenty of hardheaded U.S. citizens still believe that the swallows return to San Juan de Capistrano in California on the same day, when a look at the calendar would tell them differently.

Migrating birds never all arrive at the same time in any case. Some are early; some arrive barely in time to claim a territory and build a nest. That wise Greek philosopher Aristotle recognized this when he said, "One swallow does not make a spring." (Our proverb says, "One swallow does not make a summer.") Aristotle's point was that one piece of good luck does not mean that you will always make a success of things, and he drew on his observations of nature to illustrate it. But then Aristotle was a very unusual man for his time. He was the only Greek philosopher who bothered to study nature before pontificating about it. However, he believed that swallows hibernate in the mud during the winter, which is not true. This belief also died hard.

Legends that come down from prehistoric times tell how the barn swallow brought fire to the world. The barn swallow is a good choice for this heroic role because it has a red patch under its chin, suggesting flames, and a smoky blue head, back, and wings. The fact that it came with the warm weather gave it a magical connection with the sun. In some legends, the fire burned a hole in the middle of its tail, creating the forked shape.

During the Middle Ages, swallows were thought to bring luck to the families who lived where they built their nests. This may be the origin of the custom of putting up birdhouses for swallows. The belief is still strong from western Europe to Japan, where farmers put up boards under their eaves for the birds to nest on. Indians in the southeastern United States used to hang up hollow gourds for the purple martins.

Superstitious writers in the Middle Ages fostered the false belief that swallows knew of a magical stone or herb that could be used to restore the eyesight of its young if they should be blinded. The stone was never found by man (naturally), but the experts decided that a certain herb which they named celandine was the swallow's herb, and doctors brewed eyewashes from it.

One of the most persistent myths about a swallow dates from modern times. Back about 1964 someone measured the crop of a purple martin and estimated the number of mosquitoes it would hold if the bird ate until it could hold no more. This estimate was published, and word got around somehow that purple martins ate two thousand mosquitoes a day apiece. Mail-order merchants, spotting a good trend, began selling purple martin "apartment houses" that would accommodate a dozen or so pairs of martins, advertising them as a no-work way to eliminate mosquitoes. However, purple martins eat many other kinds of insects besides mosquitoes, and they do not seem to gorge to capacity. Martins that have been killed and examined at the height of the mosquito season were never found to have more than a few hundred mosquitoes inside them. But martins are welcome visitors anyway, for they eat wasps, beetles, flies, and locusts —all insect pests. Old-time farmers used to keep a martin house in their poultry yards, for the martins, defending their nests, would chase away crows and hawks that had come to raid the chickens. Even if the purple martins did none of these useful things, they would still be welcomed for their beauty.

SWAN

Swan is one of the oldest names for a bird in the English language. It has come down unchanged since Anglo-Saxon times. Perhaps one reason for this is the awe that the Anglo-Saxons and other old-time peoples felt for the magnificent white birds with their long, graceful necks, who passed the winter in their lands and in earliest spring disappeared toward the mysterious, unknown Northland.

The swan's name is very much alike in other Germanic languages, for instance, the Swedish *svan* and the German *Schwan*. The Romans had two names for the swan. One was *olor*, which is now seen only in scientific names. The other, *cygnus*, passed into the languages that descended from Latin. In Spanish it became *cisne*, in Italian *cigno*, in French *cygne*, and so on.

People who are particular about such things call a male swan a cob and a female a pen. The young ones are called cygnets, from the French *cygne*. No one knows the origin of "cob" or "pen," but they are handy words to throw around if you want to impress people.

Swans are related to geese and ducks, but their very long necks make it easy to tell them apart from their relatives— that and their size, for swans are the largest of all waterfowl. The swans' long necks permit them to reach down into the water for the pond weeds they feed on, for adult swans cannot dive for food. In addition to soft water plants, swans sometimes eat small water animals such as snails, freshwater clams, waterbugs, tadpoles, and fish larvae. A swan's bill is very sensitive, and it serves as a kind of feeler as the swan probes for food underwater.

Five of the world's seven species of swans live in the north of Europe, Asia, and North America. They are all pure white, except for their bills and feet. They are cold-loving birds and cannot stand heat. They stand cold well as long as they have food, and most of them breed in the Arctic. When fall comes and ponds and streams freeze over, they must move to warmer regions where there is open water. Two species of swans live south of the equator. The little black-necked swan lives in the chilly southern part of South America. The black swan, a big all-black bird, lives in Australia, where it is one of the national symbols.

Two species of swans are native to North America. One is the trumpeter swan, largest of all the swans, with a length of sixty to sixty-five inches and a wingspread of eight to nine feet. It is named for its loud, far-carrying call, which probably helps keep the swans together when they are migrating. Once common over most of the United States, the trumpeter swan was hunted until it was almost extinct. Now it is protected by law, and small flocks of trumpeters live in the Rocky Mountain region and along the west coast of Canada. Some nest in Alaska.

The whistling swan is our most common swan. About a foot shorter than the trumpeter, it nests in the far northern tundras of Alaska and Canada and spends the winter on the east and west coasts of the United States. Like the trumpeter swan, it is named for its call, which is really more of a whoop than a whistle.

The best-known swan in America is the mute swan, a native of Europe which was imported years ago to keep in parks. Millions of people who have never had a chance to see our native swans have seen these graceful birds. Some mute swans have gone wild along the east coast of the United States, and they seem to be slowly increasing and extending their range. The mute swan is named from the belief that it loses its voice when it reaches full growth. But it is not truly voiceless. Although the adults do not have the loud calls of other swans, they can make low, grunting noises, and when they are angry, they may growl and bark.

Angry swans are best avoided, for they are powerful birds and can break a man's arm with a blow of their wings. They also have pretty mean bites. But swans are generally peaceful unless they are defending their nests and young. They are devoted parents, constantly guarding their cygnets. It is believed that swans mate for life. They are long-lived birds. Some tame swans have lived eighty years.

The mute swan is the easiest of the swans to tame, and

men probably began keeping swans before the beginning of history—at first for their rich, flavorful meat and later for their beauty as well. In England an early king declared that all the swans in the kingdom belonged to him. No one cared to argue the point. For a fee, privileged people had the right to keep their own herds of swans. The birds' bills were marked with different combinations of notches to show who owned them. In the 1500's more than 900 swan marks were registered with the royal swan-keeper. All unmarked swans were considered the property of the Crown. In late summer, when the cygnets were about half grown, they were rounded up for marking. The custom was called swan-upping, for men had to chase the swans in boats and take them up from the water to mark them. It took a good deal of teamwork. First one man caught a swan by the neck with a long crook and hauled it within reach. Then his partner grabbed the swan's neck with one hand and held down its wings with a kind of wrestling hold while the first man notched the bill. It must have been painful to the cygnets, but they soon recovered. Swan-upping is still carried on in England in an annual ceremony on the Thames River near London.

Swans appear in the myths of many peoples. The Greeks believed that swans pulled the chariot in which Apollo, the sun-god, rode across the sky. They were also sacred to Aphrodite, the goddess of love. All across northern Europe and Asia, there were myths of beautiful young women who could turn into swans by putting on a magic garment of swan's skin. If a man caught one of these swan maidens without her swan robe and hid it, she had to remain in human shape and marry him. One French noble family actually claimed to be descended from a knight who had captured and married a swan-maiden. Whether many people believed them is another matter.

The Greeks had a reverse twist to the swan-maiden myth. Zeus, the leader of the gods, changed himself into a swan and made love to a beautiful mortal girl named Leda. Leda laid two eggs, which hatched into twin godlings named Castor and Pollux. The twins grew into mighty athletes and warriors—Castor was a horseman and Pollux a boxer—and took part in a number of myths. Eventually they were placed in the sky as constellations.

Europeans in the Middle Ages were very much impressed by the pure whiteness of swans. In fact, "black swan" was a proverbial expression for something that was extremely rare or did not exist at all—until black swans were discovered in Australia by a Dutch explorer in 1697.

As symbols of grace and beauty, swans were often contrasted with the clumsy, homely barnyard goose. "All his geese are swans" was an old expression for someone who always looked on the bright side of things. "All his swans are geese" meant that someone's fine promises failed to come true.

One of the strangest swan fables was about the mute swan. The Greeks believed that this bird, supposedly voiceless during its life, sang a heartbreakingly beautiful song just before it died. They passed this poetic fancy along to the Romans, and it spread through all the lands of Europe. "Swan song" was what the Greeks and Romans called the last work of a dying poet or the last song of a singer's life. In more modern times it came to mean the last performance of an actor or musician and finally the last public appearance of TV reporters.

The swan myths of ancient times almost always ended tragically. One with an upbeat ending was written in the 1800's by the famous Danish storyteller Hans Christian Andersen—"The Ugly Duckling." It was a tale of a little cygnet that lost his parents and was brought up with a flock of ducklings. Because he looked so different from the ducklings, they snubbed him and called him ugly and clumsy and played every mean trick on him that their little duckish minds could think of. The mother duck was cruel to him too. But one day the ducks looked at the ugly duckling, and—behold!—he was now a large and stately swan, more beautiful and graceful by far than they. Psychologists say that Andersen himself was the Ugly Duckling—or at least hoped that he would be transformed as the lonely cygnet was. He, too, was odd-looking and awkward, and other people were not often kind to him. But the story has brought comfort to many children who were unhappy because they were "different."

163

THRUSH

The Germans call it a *Drossel*, Swedes and Norwegians a *trast*, and Frenchmen a *grive*. Spanish-speakers say *tordo*. In English, it is a thrush, a medium-sized bird known for its sweet song. In fact, "thrush" used to be a complimentary name given to especially fine human singers.

The name "thrush" comes from *thrysce*, the Anglo-Saxon name for the bird. Actually, it referred to two different European thrushes, the song thrush, also known as the mavis, and the missel-thrush. Another old English name for the thrush was *throstle*, which is related to the German name *Drossel*. In English it hasn't been used for centuries except by poets and writers deliberately trying to be old-fashioned and quaint.

North American thrushes are a little smaller than robins. Many of them have spotted breasts. They live in forests and also backyard shrubbery and feed mainly on insects and berries. The best-known American thrushes are the wood thrush and the hermit thrush, which is the state bird of Vermont. Another common thrush is the veery, which likes to nest in damp woods. Other familiar American members of the thrush family are the robin and the bluebird.

The scientific name of the thrush is *Turdus*, which is the Latin name of the bird. The wood thrushes go by the name of *Hylocichla*, from the Greek *hyle*, "wood," plus *kichle*, "thrush." Curiously enough, *kichle* was also the Greek name for a kind of fish. Perhaps it was one of the fishes that make twittery, birdlike sounds when they are pulled up out of the water. Whether the Greeks thought of the fish as the thrush of the sea or thought of the thrush as the sweet-voiced fish of the woods is not known.

TURKEY

The turkey is a native North American bird. It was unknown
to Europeans until Spanish conquistadors brought a few
birds from Mexico back to their homeland in the 1520's.
Many people, when they saw the turkey's bald head and
bare neck, thought it was a strange new kind of giant guinea
hen. The guinea hen was then known (in England, at any
rate) as the "turkie fowle," and so the name was given to its
distant cousin from the distant New World. The guinea hen
itself had nothing to do with Turkey. Its native home was in
tropical West Africa, the region that was called the Guinea
Coast. Portuguese explorers trying to find a sea route around

Africa to India had brought guinea hens to Europe about half a century before Cortez conquered Mexico. But since Turkey then controlled most of northern Africa, "Turkish" was often used to mean "African." So the fowl from Africa became the "Turkish fowl" only to lose that title to the American bird.

There are other theories about the turkey's misfitting name. According to one, the bird's gobbling sounded like "turk-turk-turk!" In a more fanciful explanation, the name was given by Columbus' interpreter, Luis Torres. Torres was a Marrano, a Spanish Jew who had been forced to become a Catholic to save his life. When Torres first saw a strutting turkey gobbler proudly displaying his tail feathers, he exclaimed *"tukki!"*—the Hebrew name for the peacock.

In Spain, people still consider the turkey a kind of peacock and call it *pavo*, an old name for the peacock. The Portuguese named it *peru*, for they knew it came from Spain's American colonies. At that time, the Portuguese referred to all Spanish America as Peru, just as a foreigner, impressed by the size and wealth of Texas, might confuse "Texas" and "the United States."

In other countries, there was even greater confusion. The French called the turkey *poule d'inde* ("chicken of India"), or *dindon* for short, because they thought that America was a part of India. The Dutch called it *kalkoensch haan*, or "Calicut cock," because Calicut was the leading city in India for trading with Europeans. Later, this name was shortened to *kalkoen* (pronounced kahl-KOON) and was taken up by the Swedes, Danes, and Norwegians, who did a lot of trading with the Dutch. The Germans also called the turkey a Calicut chicken but later switched to *Truthahn*, for which there is no really good explanation.

The turkey belongs to the chicken family, like the pheasant, peacock, guinea hen, grouse, quail, and other edible birds too numerous to mention. There are two species of turkey. One, the common wild turkey, is the ancestor of all our domestic breeds. It formerly ranged over most of the United States east of the Great Plains, in the Southwest, and down to the south of Mexico. The male turkey, also called the tom, gobbler, or cock, has bright-red, fleshy wattles and a peculiar inflatable growth on his forehead. When limp, it dangles down along his beak like a misplaced tentacle. When the male is excited, as when challenging other males in a mating contest, it swells with blood and stands out like a horn. Male turkeys seem to go through their mating displays more to impress each other than to impress the females. A hen turkey must actually lie down in front of her chosen male to get his attention.

The other species is the ocellated turkey, which lives in Honduras, Guatemala, and the Yucatán Peninsula in southeastern Mexico. The ocellated turkey looks a little like a peacock, with its very long tail feathers ornamented with bright-colored "eye spots." It also lacks the wattles of the common gobbler. But on its naked, blue head it has red, wartlike growths that no true peacock would be caught dead with. This would probably be the turkey that Luis Torres mistook for a peacock, if the story were true.

Wherever the wild turkey was found in North America, the Indians made good use of it. Not only did they hunt it for food, but they used the feathers for decorations and made whistles out of the bones. Few tribes tried to domesticate turkeys, but down in Mexico the Aztecs raised the common turkey and the Mayas raised ocellated turkeys. Some of the settled Pueblo tribes of the southwestern United States raised turkeys too.

The Spanish conquistadors of Cortez' expedition tasted turkey in Mexico and found it good. It was not long before turkeys were seen in Spain and then in other parts of Europe. Half a century before the Pilgrims sailed for America, Englishmen were already feasting on turkey at Christmas. When the Pilgrims and other early settlers arrived in New England they were overjoyed to find wild turkeys just like the tame English ones.

Today we eat turkey to commemorate the first Thanksgiving, the feast which the Pilgrims held to celebrate their first harvest. Yet there was no mention of turkey in any records left by the Pilgrims of that first Thanksgiving celebration. Deer, duck, goose, shellfish, leeks, watercress, wild plums, and wine made from wild grapes were all listed—but no turkey. So turkey for Thanksgiving may really be a custom taken over from Britain. As a matter of fact, Thanksgiving itself was not a national holiday until 1863, two hundred and forty-two years after the first one was celebrated.

Like the Indians, the early settlers often ate turkey, until the woods were all cut down to make way for farmland. Then the wild turkeys disappeared, for wild turkeys need forests to live in. Afterward it became traditional to eat turkey only at Thanksgiving and Christmastime, until turkey farmers decided to change this habit by advertising. At the same time, government scientists were breeding smaller turkeys, for the American way of life had changed greatly. Most Americans now lived in cities or towns, instead of on farms, and their families were smaller. Their ovens seldom had room for one of the thirty-pound turkeys that once were the farmer's pride, and even if they did, it was too much for the average family to eat, even if Grandpa and Grandma and Uncle Fred and Aunt Alice and Great-Aunt Hilda and a crew of cousins were invited to help. So now we enjoy our smaller turkeys at any time of the year.

The turkey played such an important part in American life that it became a part of many expressions. "Talking turkey" meant getting down to business or talking straight from the shoulder, with no frills. "Strutting like a turkey cock," "red as a turkey cock," and "swelled up like a turkey gobbler" described vanity, anger, and pomposity. In show-business language, a "turkey" was a show that flopped. A popular dance of the early 1900's was called the "turkey trot" because the dancers moved with little, jerky steps like a turkey's.

In the myths of the Indians, the turkey was a hero that helped in the creation of the world. It showed people how to raise corn and other crops, and fought against evil spirits like the Owl. In one tale, it taught the Indians to use tobacco and even how to roll cigarettes! The turkey had a more sinister side, too. In the beliefs of some tribes, sorcerers used to turn themselves into wild turkeys and prowl around Indian villages at night, alert for any chance to do harm.

Benjamin Franklin once proposed that the turkey should be the national bird of the United States. He pointed out that the bald eagle was a lazy, rather cowardly bird that stole from other birds and would even eat carrion rather than hunt for himself. The eagle was also lousy. Furthermore, said Franklin, the eagle was really a foreign bird, for it appeared in the crests of many European rulers—just the kind of thing the United States was fighting against.

The turkey was a courageous fighter, fended for itself, and was a native American bird. Furthermore, it was good to eat, which the eagle certainly was not. Had Franklin won his argument, our dollar bills might now bear the picture of a majestic turkey with outspread wings, clutching an olive branch and a bundle of arrows in its talons!

VULTURE

Nobody loves the vulture. The bird's ugly, naked head and neck and its habit of eating dead bodies fill most people with disgust and loathing. Yet the despised vulture plays a very important part in nature's cleanup squad, disposing of dead animals that would otherwise rot and spread disease.

Vultures' ancestors were once birds of prey, and the vultures are still classed together with hawks and eagles. But millions of years ago the ancestors of the vultures began to specialize in scavenging rather than hunting their own food. This specialty left its marks on them. The most noticeable is the naked head and neck. In feeding on a carcass, a vulture often has to plunge its head and neck deep inside, getting

172

them covered with filth. These are the only parts of its body that the vulture cannot reach with its beak to clean them. A bird with feathers on its head and neck would soon be matted down with filth and would eventually succumb to disease. But the filth does not stick easily on the vulture's bare, scaly skin, and what does adhere soon dries up and falls off. In addition, the lack of feathers lets the sun's rays disinfect the vulture's head and neck.

Another mark of the carrion eater is the vulture's weak bill and claws. Since vultures do not have to subdue living prey, they did not need a powerful bite or grip. Some species of vultures do hunt occasionally, but they prefer very weak prey like young birds, toads, and baby mammals.

Vultures are patient "hunters," circling tirelessly in the sky for hours on end until they spy a dead or dying animal. When a vulture finds a carcass, it comes swooping down, followed by other vultures from miles around, for vultures seem to watch each other as closely as they watch the ground. The vultures stand around in a ring at a safe distance, waiting to make sure the animal is truly and safely dead. Finally some bold vulture bites into the carcass, and a free-for-all ensues as the vultures squabble over first turn at the banquet. The larger and more aggressive vultures crowd the weaker ones away with threatening hisses and menacing gestures and settle down to dine with a very hearty appetite. Vultures have been known to eat so much that they could not fly away afterward. However, they must often go a long time between meals, so this greedy behavior helps in their survival.

"Vulture" comes from the Latin *vultur*, which comes from the word *vellere*, "to pull at," which describes very well the vulture's table manners. As far back as Roman times, "vulture" has also been an epithet for a greedy, heartless person. Yet vultures in truth do such a valuable job of cleaning up that they are protected by law in many countries, including the United States.

American vultures are very distantly related to the vultures of the Old World, although following the same way of life has made them look very much alike. The old-world vultures, so many scientists think, share a common ancestor with the eagles, which also do a good bit of scavenging. The American vultures are a far older family.

The giant of them all is the condor of the Andes. Largest of the soaring birds, it reaches a length of four feet and a wingspread of ten feet. Yet for all its size it weighs only twenty to twenty-five pounds, about the same as a big supermarket turkey. The California condor is almost as big. Ugly to look at on the ground, it is majestic in flight. But this harmless bird is almost extinct. Only about sixty breeding pairs are left, in a desolate mountain section of southern California.

The most common vultures in North America are the turkey vulture and the black vulture, both known as buzzards. The black vulture is named for its color, and its scientific name, *Coragyps atratus*, means "raven vulture dressed in black." Black vultures used to scavenge in the streets of Charleston, South Carolina, and other Southern cities, until modern garbage departments took their living away. They still raid garbage dumps in some communities.

The turkey vulture was named for its size and because its small-beaked red head looks a bit like a turkey's. Its scientific name, *Cathartes aura*, means "golden purifier." The turkey vulture ranges from southern Canada to the Straits of Magellan, but in the United States it is commonest in the

South. The turkey vulture and black vulture have adapted well to man's mechanized world. They have found a wonderful free lunch counter along the highways, where so many rabbits, cats, dogs, and other animals are killed by speeding cars. Sometimes the vultures are killed, too, but that is a risk that does not appear to bother them. Otherwise, they would be more careful about getting out of the way.

Vultures have a keener sense of smell than most other birds, and experts have argued for years whether they find their food by smell or sight. Turkey vultures apparently use smell at least some of the time, for in tests they have been able to find meat that was covered over by leaves. Black vultures, on the other hand, always fail these tests. One black vulture even attacked a live skunk, undismayed by the skunk's malodorous spray, which hardly indicates a sensitive "nose." In one experiment, scientists laid out a well-ripened, smelly carcass in a field and covered it over so that it could be scented but not seen. The vultures ignored it. But when the scientists laid out a large picture of the carcass, the vultures came flocking down to it and even tried to eat the picture!

WARBLER

"To warble" means to sing in a soft, melodious fashion, with trill and quavers and variations. In Europe there is a family of small dull-colored birds that sings this way, so they were named "warblers." The name was later given to a group of American birds that are not related to the European warblers and have nothing in common with them except small size and a diet of insects. Many of the American warblers are bright-colored (at least, the males are in breeding time), with yellow the predominant color. Most of them sing poorly—their voices are thin and weak. Some sound like buzzing insects. To avoid confusion, many ornithologists call the American warblers wood warblers. The "wood" is an accurate description, at least, for they nest in forests.

Though they are only about the size of sparrows, wood warblers migrate hundreds of miles to their winter homes in Mexico, Central America, and the West Indies. Flying at night, they are often lured to their death by lighthouses and aircraft beacons. Others crash into bridges, TV towers, and tall buildings. So far the warblers have survived these losses. We may hope they continue to do so.

WHIPPOORWILL

The whippoorwill is a bird that is often heard but very seldom seen, for it rests by day and hunts by night. During the day it sits motionless on the ground in the woods, its mottled gray and brown feathers making it look like a patch of dead leaves. After sundown the whippoorwill flits around on its long, pointed wings, catching insects in its gaping mouth and loudly uttering a call that sounds like "WHIP-poor-WILL!" Early settlers in America named the bird for its call. Some whippoorwills seem never to get tired of calling. One naturalist woke up at three in the morning and heard a whippoorwill outside his window. He began to count the

"WHIP-poor-WILLS!", having nothing better to do, and got up to 1,088 when the bird stopped for a half-minute breather. The whippoorwill gave 398 more calls, flew a little farther away, and kept on with its concert until the exhausted naturalist fell asleep again.

Whippoorwills are birds that have evolved into flying insect traps. Their huge mouths scoop up any insects in front of them as they fly through the night air, and long, stiff bristles around their mouths help funnel insects in. Their beaks are very small and weak, since they are not needed for seizing prey or cracking seeds. Whippoorwills' legs and feet are also very small and weak, and the birds very seldom use them for walking. If they want to move to another spot, they will fly, even if it is only a couple of feet away.

Whippoorwills belong to a family of birds called the nightjars, named from the call of a European species that is so loud that it "jars the night." The nightjars are all insect eaters, and they all look and behave remarkably alike. Many of them are named for their calls, like the chuck-will's-

widow, which lives in the eastern half of the United States, and the poorwill, which lives in the West. The whippoorwill itself is found from New Brunswick, Canada, to Florida and as far west as the Canadian province of Saskatchewan. It is also found in the Southwest. The poorwill is the only bird that is known to hibernate. In the fall, some poorwills creep into crevices and holes in canyon walls and almost literally "turn off." Their body temperature drops way down, they breathe hardly at all, and their digestive system stops working. They stay in this state until the weather warms up again in spring and brings more insects for them to eat. The poorwills that do not hibernate have to migrate south.

Whippoorwills and their relatives belong to a group of birds called the goatsuckers. This name was fastened on them by the ancient Greeks, who saw European nightjars flitting around the goat pens in the evening with their mouths wide open. The birds were hunting for insects, of course, but the Greeks, who loved weird and fantastic stories, thought that they were waiting for a chance to suck milk from the goats' udders. The scientific name of the family, Caprimulgiformes, is Latin for "goat-milker-shaped birds." Despite the superstition, none of the birds steals milk, and they do a great deal of good in disposing of mosquitoes and other harmful insects.

Strange as it may seem, the closest relatives of the goatsucker birds are the owls. Millions of years ago they had a common ancestor, which became a nighttime hunter to get away from the competition of daytime hunters like hawks. The owls specialized in preying on small mammals and birds, while the goatsuckers took advantage of the huge swarms of insects that are out at night.

As birds of the night, with weird and sometimes terrifying

calls, whippoorwills and their relatives were often thought to have supernatural powers, and sometimes to be in league with the devil. In backwoods districts of America, people believed (and some still may) that if a whippoorwill lit on the roof of a house, someone in the neighborhood would soon die. Some believed that whippoorwills would gather around the house of a dying person, waiting to snatch the soul as it left the body and carry it off.

But to nature lovers, the whippoorwill's call is one of the things that adds interest to a summer night.

WOODPECKER

The woodpecker is one of the most aptly named birds, for it spends most of its waking hours pecking holes in trees to get at the grubs and insects it lives on. But it did not get its present name until the 1500's. Before then it went by a variety of other names. The Anglo-Saxon name for the woodpecker was *higora*, which was later twisted into *hickwall* and *highwall*. Another old name was *speck*, which may have carried the idea of a pointed instrument—the bird's chisel-like bill. In the Middle Ages still another name for the woodpecker was *wodehake*, or "wood-hack."

The woodpecker's pecking seems to have impressed practically everyone. The ancient Greeks had at least three names for the woodpecker: *pelekas,* or "ax-bird," *dryoko-laptes,* or "tree-chisel," and *dryokopos,* or "tree-splitter." The Romans called it *picus,* which is distantly related to our English words "pick" and "peck." Spanish-speakers call it *carpintero,* or "carpenter."

The Romans had a legend about a woodland god named Picus who had the bad luck to have the famed enchantress Circe fall in love with him. Unfortunately, she did not appeal to Picus. When he turned her down, she comforted her wounded heart by turning him into a woodpecker and condemning him to spend the rest of his life pecking at trees.

Scientists have a different story. More than 50,000,000 years ago the woodpeckers' ancestors discovered a good source of food in the grubs and bugs that tunnel beneath the bark of trees. Not only were they a good source of nutrition, but other birds could not reach them, so the woodpeckers had no rivals for their food supply. Over thousands of years the woodpeckers evolved to take advantage of this specialized food source. Their bills became strong and sharp-pointed, for chiseling into wood. Their skulls became heavy, to take the shock of the bill's hammerlike blows. Their neck muscles became strong and wiry to deliver those blows. Woodpeckers' tongues grew long and barbed at the end, to snake down into an insect tunnel and impale the insect or grub. Their feet developed strong, hooked claws to dig into the bark and give them a firm hold as they pecked away— without this hold, a woodpecker would knock itself off the tree each time it gave a hard peck. Their tail feathers became stiff and sturdy, to prop them upright on the tree trunk. With such a set of equipment, the woodpecker could hardly miss being a success.

Woodpeckers usually start their insect hunt near the base

of a tree and work up the trunk, spiraling around it to cover all parts. When they reach the top, they fly down to the bottom of another tree and start again. Woodpeckers have a peculiar up-and-down flight. They fly for several wing beats, fold up their wings and coast downward, and then regain altitude with another series of wing beats.

There are woodpeckers on every continent of the world except Australia and Antarctica. There are more than twenty species in North America, counting the flickers, which spend a good deal of time on the ground hunting for ants, and the sapsuckers, which drill holes in tree bark to feed on the sap that oozes out. Small insects gather around the sap holes, and the sapsucker also eats these. The yellow-bellied sapsucker, named for its pale-yellow underside, is common in apple orchards. Despite all the holes they drill, sapsuckers do not seem to damage the trees, and they do some good by eating caterpillars, moths, and grasshoppers.

The most familiar woodpecker of North America is probably the downy woodpecker, a friendly sparrow-sized bird that is common around suburbs and farmland. The hairy woodpecker, which looks just like the downy but is twice the size, is also fairly common, but it is shyer and less often seen.

The California woodpecker, common along most of the west coast, drills holes in trees and stores acorns in them for future use. It usually selects dead or dying trees for storage racks, so this habit does no harm. But sometimes it uses a telephone pole, weakening it and shortening its life. This does not make it popular with utility companies.

The largest American woodpecker was the great ivory-billed woodpecker, which reached a foot and a half in length. It is probably extinct, though some bird lovers claim to have sighted one—or at least heard its calls—in impenetrable Southern swamps. The ivorybill was a bird of deep woods with large, old trees. It could not survive when the woods were cut down. The largest woodpecker known to be alive in North America is the fifteen-inch pileated woodpecker, sometimes known as the Lord God woodpecker because of its size.

Most of the American woodpeckers are black and white, and the males have the well-known red head. Some, like the downy, have only a small red patch. Others have a big patch or crest. One, the redheaded woodpecker, has its whole head and neck red.

Primitive people in Europe used to believe that the woodpecker was a thunderbird. By making a thundering noise on trees, they reasoned, it brought on real thunder and the rain that crops and pastures had to have. The Greeks made the woodpecker sacred to Zeus, who controlled the thunder and rain. The woodpeckers would surely have been surprised if they had known of this.

WREN

An old European legend tells how all the birds held a convention to choose a king. After much screeching and ruffling of feathers, and some threatening behavior from the more powerful birds, it was decided that the bird who could fly highest would be king. Up flapped the birds, one after another. Some of the feathered contestants, who were weak fliers, could get only a few yards into the air. Some, like the ostrich, didn't even get off the ground. But most of them managed to reach a pretty fair altitude. Then it was the turn of the champions, as one bird after another reached its ceiling and could go no farther. Finally, only the eagle was left, soaring high above the other birds. Triumphantly the eagle opened its powerful, hooked bill to announce its victory. But the eagle's victory scream was drowned out by a loud burst of song from above. It was the wren, who had hitched a ride on the eagle's back and then, rested and full of energy, fluttered a few feet higher than the eagle to win the kingship.

This story is not at all out of character for the wren, a tiny but bold and resourceful bird with enough vocal power for a bird three times its size. The wren bossily drives other birds off its territory, singing loud, threatening songs as it buzzes them. Yet it seldom shows itself in the open and prefers to skulk around in underbrush, hedgerows, and rock crevices.

Most wrens are small, brownish birds. The house wren measures only four to four and a half inches from beak to tail tip, and the winter wren is even smaller, with an average size of three and a quarter inches. The giant of the family is the eight-inch cactus wren, which lives in the desert lands of the southwestern United States and northern Mexico. Wrens are easy to recognize by their habit of cocking their tail feathers up in the air.

Wrens are insect eaters, and many species move south when fall comes. The winter wren is one of the species that somehow finds food in the North during the lean winter months. Rather rare in the United States and southern Canada, it is the only wren found in Europe.

The name "wren" comes from the Anglo-Saxon *wrenna*, which doesn't seem to have any other meaning. But in some European languages the wren has been named for its domineering attitude toward other birds. In German it is named *Zaunkönig*, or "king of the hedge." The Dutch call it *winterkoning*, or "winter king," since it stays around through the winter. The French name is *roitelet*, "tiny king," and one of the Spanish names for the wren is *rey de zarza*, or "king of the brambles." But the Swedes call it *gärdsmyg*, meaning "fence sneak," from its habit of stealthily scurrying through underbrush along fence rows and hiding in cracks in stone walls.

The wren's scientific name, *Troglodytes*, means "cave-dweller." It was suggested partly by the wren's furtive habits, and partly by the fact that many species of wrens build their nests in hollow trees, rock crevices, old woodpecker holes, hollows under tree roots, and even empty wasps' nests. Even the wrens that build their nests in the open make solid, closed-in structures with an opening in the side, rather like a small cave built of grass and twigs. Most wrens build their nest on the ground or less than a foot above it. The cactus wren nests out in the open—among the long, sharp spines of a tall cactus plant, where it is safe from predators. The marsh wren builds ball-shaped nests of grass attached to reeds. The male builds several extra "dummy nests" and sleeps in one of them, apart from the female and young.

Male wrens do most of the nest building in all species, and they all have the habit of building extra nests. The nest built for the female and young is usually much more sturdily built and better hidden than the dummy nests. Some scientists believe that the purpose of the dummy nests is to fool predators; others think the male birds are gripped by a building instinct that has gone a bit out of control.

In most countries where they are found, wrens are loved for their cheery song. In England they are called Jenny Wren or Kitty Wren, which are also nicknames for small, cheerful, bustling girls. Yet in England and Ireland boys used to go out to the country and kill wrens on St. Stephen's

Day (December 26), hang their bodies on a bush, and parade them around through the towns singing a special song and begging for money. The "wren boys" still go out in some places, dressed in outlandish clothes and with their faces blackened, though fortunately they have stopped killing wrens.

Scholars trace the custom back to an ancient pagan religion, far older than Christianity, in which the wren was sacred to the earth gods. The wren was also supposed to have brought fire to man and got its feathers scorched in the process. That would explain why the wren boys blackened their faces.

Some of these ancient beliefs lingered on in folklore in strange disguises. In parts of Europe, the wren was thought to be in league with the devil; in other parts it was said to be a pet of the Virgin Mary. The Irish had a legend about a saint who lost his temper at a wren who ate his pet fly. He laid a curse on the bird and all its descendants, dooming them to live forever in empty houses dripping with dampness and to be hunted without mercy by children and young persons. In the Ozark Mountains of Arkansas and Missouri, old backcountry people used to believe that wrens had a deadly poisonous bite because they ate so many spiders.

There are fifty-nine species of wrens, all of them native to the New World. Only one, the winter wren, is found in Europe and Asia. (In England, the name "wren" is also used for small birds of an unrelated family.) Wrens have adapted to almost every kind of habitat: woodland, farmland, arid desert, sodden marshland, rocky mountainsides, precipitous canyon walls, and suburban backyards. Wrens will nest in birdhouses if they are put up. If they cannot find a better location, they have been known to use mailboxes, empty tin cans, and junked cars or tractors. Wrens also like to sleep under cover. Sometimes they have been found asleep in the pockets of shirts hung out to dry.

The cactus wren is the state bird of Arizona, and the Carolina wren is the state bird of South Carolina.

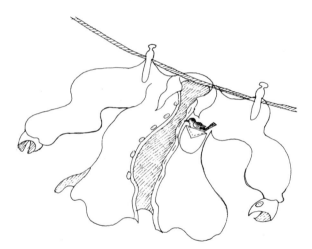

Selected Bibliography

Austin, Oliver L., Jr., *Birds of the World*. New York, Golden Press, 1961.

Armstrong, Edward A., *The Folklore of Birds*. Gloucester, Mass., Peter Smith, 1964.

Burt, Harold E., *The Psychology of Birds*. New York, Macmillan, Inc., 1967.

Gruson, Edward S., *Words for Birds*. New York, Quadrangle/The New York Times Book Co., 1972.

Pearson, T. Gilbert, ed., *Birds of America*. Garden City, L. I., Garden City Publishing Co., 1936.

Peterson, Roger Tory, *The Birds*. New York, Time-Life Books, 1968.

Randolph, Vance, *Ozark Superstitions*. New York, Dover Publications, Inc., 1964.

Robbins, Chandler S.; Bruun, Bertel; and Zim, Herbert A., *Birds of North America*. New York, Golden Press, 1966.

About the Author

Peter Limburg was graduated from Yale University and earned an MA in U.S. history at Columbia University. His fascination with word origins has lead him to write three other books on the subject, *What's in the Names of Fruits?*, *What's in the Names of Antique Weapons?* and *What's in the Names of Flowers?* He also writes a column for *Science World* Magazine on the subject of words.

Mr. Limburg enjoys gardening, hiking, and fishing. He and his wife, Margareta, and their four children make their home in Bedford, New York.

About the Artist

Tom Huffman has illustrated several books for children including *Your Silent Language* and *Wrapped for Eternity: The Story of the Egyptian Mummy* for which he received an award for graphics from the Printing Industries of America. His work also appears in national magazines.

Mr. Huffman makes his home in New York City.